PARISH MASS BOOK

YEAR A – Volume 2

OUR LADY OF MOUNT CARMEL AND ST. JOSEPH R.C. CHURCH BATTERSEA PARK

McCRIMMONS
Great Wakering Essex UK

This edition first published in 2014
Published by McCrimmon Publishing Co Ltd
10–12 High Street, Great Wakering, Essex, SS3 0EQ, UK
Telephone (01702) 218 956   Fax (01702) 216082
info@mccrimmons.com   www.mccrimmons.com

Compilation and layout
© Copyright 2014, McCrimmon Publishing Co Ltd

ISBN 978-0-85597-726-9   A5 Standard edition
ISBN 978-0-85597-727-6   A4 Large-print edition

Concordat cum Originali   Jane Porter

Nihil obstat   Rt Rev Mgr David Manson
     Censor Deputatus, 2014

Imprimatur   + Rt Rev Thomas McMahon
     Bishop of Brentwood

Approved for use in the dioceses of England and Wales.
Permission granted for distribution in the dioceses of Scotland and Ireland.

Acknowledgements

Excerpts from the English translation and chants of *The Roman Missal* © 2010, International Commission on English in the Liturgy Corporation (ICEL); the English translation of *General Introduction from Lectionary for Mass* © 1969, 1981, 1997, ICEL; excerpts from the English translation of *Holy Communion & Worship of the Eucharist outside Mass* © 1974, ICEL; excerpts from the English translation of *Rite of Christian Initiation of Adults* © 1985, ICEL; excerpts from the English translation of *Ceremonial of Bishops* © 1989, ICEL. All rights reserved.

Further copyright acknowledgements are found on page 4.

Project management and typesetting: Patrick Geary.

The publishers wish to express their thanks to the following for their help in the preparation of this volume: Patrick Geary, Martin Foster and Jane Porter.

Cover design: Nick Snode.

Cover illustration by The Benedictine Sisters of Turvey Abbey.
The four letters of this Christogram represent a traditional abbreviation of the Greek words for 'Jesus Christ' (i.e., the first and last letters of each of the words – 'ΙΗCΟΥC ΧΡΙCΤΟC' (Iesoùs Christòs).

Typeset in ITC Stone Serif and ITC Stone Sans.
Printed and bound by CPI Group (UK) Ltd, Croydon, CR0 4YY   B/AD

CONTENTS

MUSIC

Some music is printed in the *Order of Mass* and in the propers. A fuller set of chants for the *Order of Mass* is found in the section *Music for the Order of Mass*. Cross-references to these chants are provided in the *Order of Mass*.

Consistent with the approach used in the Altar edition of *The Roman Missal*, the music of the chants is notated in order to avoid the use of key signatures. This does not preclude the chants being sung at a different pitch. Indeed, a pitch should be chosen which is comfortable for the Priest, Deacon, reader, cantor and assembly, in order to aid full participation in the liturgy.

ORDER OF MASS

In celebrating the Eucharist, the people of God assemble as the body of Christ to fulfil the Lord's command: 'do this in memory of me' (Luke 22:19).

At the Last Supper the Lord gathered his disciples, he spoke to them, took bread and wine, broke the bread, and gave them the Bread of life and the Cup of eternal salvation. In the Eucharist the Church to this day makes Christ's memorial and celebrates his presence in the same sequence of actions: we gather in Christ's name, in the Liturgy of the Word we listen as the word of God is proclaimed and explained, in the Liturgy of the Eucharist, we take bread and wine, give thanks, and receive the Body and Blood of Christ.

Christ is always present in his Church, particularly in its liturgical celebrations. In the celebration of Mass, Christ is really present in the very liturgical assembly gathered in his name, in the person of the minister who acts in the person of Christ, in the proclamation of his word and under the Eucharistic species. This presence of Christ under the appearance of bread and wine is called real, not to exclude other ways in which Christ is present, but because it is real *par excellence*.

cf Celebrating the Mass nn 18–19, 22;
General Instruction of the Roman Missal n 27;
Holy Communion and the Worship of the Eucharist
Outside Mass n 6.

OUTLINE OF THE ORDER OF MASS

INTRODUCTORY RITES
Opening Song
Greeting
Penitential Act
Gloria (omitted during Advent and Lent)
Opening Prayer

LITURGY OF THE WORD
First Reading
Responsorial Psalm
Second Reading
Gospel Acclamation
Gospel
Homily
Profession of Faith
Prayer of the Faithful

LITURGY OF THE EUCHARIST
Preparation of Gifts
Prayer over the Gifts
EUCHARISTIC PRAYER

COMMUNION RITE
The Lord's Prayer
Rite of Peace
Lamb of God
Holy Communion
Prayer after Communion

CONCLUDING RITES
Blessing
Dismissal

INTRODUCTORY RITES

> *Where two or three are gathered in my name,*
> *there am I in their midst.*
> *(Matthew 18:20)*
>
> The Introductory Rites help the faithful come together as one, to establish communion and to prepare themselves properly to listen to the word of God and to celebrate the Eucharist worthily.

ENTRANCE SONG
`ALL STAND`

While the Entrance Song is sung, the Priest approaches the altar with the ministers and venerates it.

SIGN OF THE CROSS
`▷ Music p 205`

All make the Sign of the Cross as the Priest says

Priest: In the name of the Father, and of the Son, and of the Holy Spirit.
People: **Amen.**

GREETING

Priest: The grace of our Lord Jesus Christ,
           and the love of God,
           and the communion of the Holy Spirit
           be with you all.

or

Priest: Grace to you and peace from God our Father
           and the Lord Jesus Christ.

or

Priest: The Lord be with you.
People: **And with your spirit.**

A Bishop will say:

Bishop: Peace be with you
People: **And with your spirit.**

The Priest, or a Deacon, or another minister, may very briefly introduce the faithful to the Mass of the day.

PENITENTIAL ACT

Because of its emphasis on Easter and Baptism, the Blessing and Sprinkling of Water (page 62) may take place on Sundays, especially in Easter Time. When it is used it replaces the Penitential Act.

Otherwise, one of the following three forms of the Penitential Act is used. Each Penitential Act begins with the invitation to the faithful by the Priest:

        Brethren (brothers and sisters), let us acknowledge our sins,
        and so prepare ourselves to celebrate the sacred mysteries.

A brief pause for silence follows.

On certain days during the Church's year, for example Palm Sunday and the Easter Vigil, and during certain other celebrations, for example a Funeral Mass, Rite of Entry into the Catechumenate or Baptism, the Introductory Rites take a different form.

Penitential Act A

All: I confess to almighty God
          and to you, my brothers and sisters,
          that I have greatly sinned,
          in my thoughts and in my words,
          in what I have done and in what I have failed to do,

All strike their breast.

          through my fault, through my fault,
          through my most grievous fault;
          therefore I ask blessed Mary ever-Virgin,
          all the Angels and Saints,
          and you, my brothers and sisters,
          to pray for me to the Lord our God.

Penitential Act B   ▷ *Music p 206*

Priest: Have mercy on us, O Lord.
People: **For we have sinned against you.**

Priest: Show us, O Lord, your mercy.
People: **And grant us your salvation.**

Penitential Act C   ▷ *Music p 206*

After the silence the Priest or another minister invokes the gracious works of the Lord
to which he invites the Kyrie eleison invocations, in sequence, as in the example below:

Priest or minister: You were sent to heal the contrite of heart:
                      Lord, have mercy.   *or*   Kyrie, eleison.
People: **Lord, have mercy.**   *or*   **Kyrie, eleison.**

Priest or minister: You came to call sinners:
                      Christ, have mercy.   *or*   Christe, eleison.
People: **Christ, have mercy.** *or*   **Christe, eleison.**

Priest or minister: You are seated at the right hand of the Father to intercede for us:
                      Lord, have mercy.   *or*   Kyrie, eleison.
People: **Lord, have mercy.**   *or*   **Kyrie, eleison.**

The absolution by the Priest follows all of the options above

Priest: May almighty God have mercy on us,   ▷ *Music p 207*
          forgive us our sins,
          and bring us to everlasting life.
All: **Amen.**

KYRIE

▷ Music p 207

The Kyrie, eleison (Lord, have mercy) invocations may follow:

Lord, have mercy. **Lord, have mercy.**		Kyrie, eleison. **Kyrie, eleison.**
Christ, have mercy. **Christ, have mercy.**	*or*	Christe, eleison. **Christe, eleison.**
Lord, have mercy. **Lord, have mercy.**		Kyrie, eleison. **Kyrie, eleison.**

GLORIA

▷ Music p 208

When indicated this hymn is sung or said:

All: **Glory to God in the highest,
and on earth peace to people of good will.
We praise you,
we bless you,
we adore you,
we glorify you,
we give you thanks for your great glory,
Lord God, heavenly King,
O God, almighty Father.**

**Lord Jesus Christ, Only Begotten Son,
Lord God, Lamb of God, Son of the Father,
you take away the sins of the world,
     have mercy on us;
you take away the sins of the world,
     receive our prayer;
you are seated at the right hand of the Father,
     have mercy on us.**

**For you alone are the Holy One,
you alone are the Lord,
you alone are the Most High,
Jesus Christ,
with the Holy Spirit,
in the glory of God the Father.
Amen.**

COLLECT

▷ Proper

Priest: Let us pray.

All pray in silence for a while. Then the Priest says the Collect, to which the people respond:

People: **Amen.**

ALL SIT

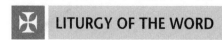 **LITURGY OF THE WORD**

Did not our hearts burn within us as he spoke to us
and explained the Scriptures to us?
(cf Luke 24:32)

In the Liturgy of the Word the assembly listens with hearts burning as the Lord speaks to it again and it responds with words of praise and petition.

By hearing the word proclaimed in worship, the faithful again enter into the unending dialogue between God and the covenant people, a dialogue sealed in the sharing of the Eucharistic food and drink. The proclamation of the word is thus integral to the Mass and at its very centre.

Celebrating the Mass nn 19, 152

FIRST READING ▷ Proper

The reader goes to the ambo and proclaims the First Reading, while all sit and listen.

To indicate the end of the reading, the reader acclaims:

Reader: The word of the Lord. ▷ Music p 209
All: **Thanks be to God.**

Following this reading, and the other readings it is appropriate to have a brief time of quiet as those present take the word of God to heart and begin to prepare a prayerful response to what they have heard.

RESPONSORIAL PSALM

The psalmist or cantor sings or says the Psalm, with the people making the response.

SECOND READING

On Sundays and certain other days there is a second reading.

To indicate the end of the reading, the reader acclaims:

Reader: The word of the Lord. ▷ Music p 209
All: **Thanks be to God.**

GOSPEL ACCLAMATION **ALL STAND**

The assembly stands for the Gospel Acclamation to welcome the Gospel.
The Gospel Acclamation may not be omitted where there is more than one reading before the Gospel.

The Gospel Acclamation is

Alleluia

GOSPEL

The assembly remains standing in honour of the Gospel reading,
the high point of the Liturgy of the Word.

At the ambo the Deacon, or the Priest, sings or says:

Deacon or Priest: The Lord be with you.   ▷ *Music p 209*

All: **And with your spirit.**

Deacon or Priest: A reading from the holy Gospel according to N.

The Deacon or Priest makes the Sign of the Cross on the book and, together with the people,
on his forehead, lips, and breast.

All: **Glory to you, O Lord.**

At the end of the Gospel, the Deacon, or the Priest, acclaims:

Deacon or Priest: The Gospel of the Lord.

All: **Praise to you, Lord Jesus Christ.**

ALL SIT

HOMILY

The Homily is preached by a Priest or Deacon on all Sundays and Holydays of Obligation.
On other days, it is recommended.

At the end of the Homily it is appropriate for there to be a brief silence for recollection.

ALL STAND

PROFESSION OF FAITH

On Sundays and Solemnities, the Profession of Faith will follow.

In Masses that include acceptance into the order of catechumens and in ritual Masses for the election
or enrolment of names or for the Scrutinies, the Profession of Faith may be omitted.

On most occasions the form used is that of the Niceno-Constantinopolitan Creed.
However, especially during Lent and Easter Time, the Apostles' Creed (page 12) may be used.

If the Profession of Faith is not said, the Prayer of the Faithful follows.

Niceno-Constantinopolitan Creed   ▷ *Music p 210*

I believe in one God,
the Father almighty,
maker of heaven and earth,
of all things visible and invisible.

I believe in one Lord Jesus Christ,
the Only Begotten Son of God,
born of the Father before all ages.
God from God, Light from Light,
true God from true God,
begotten, not made, consubstantial with the Father;

through him all things were made.
For us men and for our salvation
he came down from heaven,

At the words that follow, up to and including 'and became man', all bow.

and by the Holy Spirit was incarnate of the Virgin Mary,
and became man.

For our sake he was crucified under Pontius Pilate,
he suffered death and was buried,
and rose again on the third day
in accordance with the Scriptures.
He ascended into heaven
and is seated at the right hand of the Father.
He will come again in glory
to judge the living and the dead
and his kingdom will have no end.

I believe in the Holy Spirit, the Lord, the giver of life,
who proceeds from the Father and the Son,
who with the Father and the Son is adored and glorified,
who has spoken through the prophets.

I believe in one, holy, catholic and apostolic Church.
I confess one Baptism for the forgiveness of sins
and I look forward to the resurrection of the dead
and the life of the world to come. Amen.

THE APOSTLES' CREED

Instead of the Niceno-Constantinopolitan Creed, the Apostles' Creed, may be used.

I believe in God,
the Father almighty
Creator of heaven and earth,
and in Jesus Christ, his only Son, our Lord,

At the words that follow, up to and including 'the Virgin Mary', all bow.

who was conceived by the Holy Spirit,
born of the Virgin Mary,
suffered under Pontius Pilate,
was crucified, died and was buried;
he descended into hell;
on the third day he rose again from the dead;
he ascended into heaven,
and is seated at the right hand of God the Father almighty;
from there he will come to judge the living and the dead.

I believe in the Holy Spirit,
the holy catholic Church,
the communion of saints,
the forgiveness of sins,
the resurrection of the body,
and life everlasting. Amen.

PRAYER OF THE FAITHFUL

Enlightened and moved by God's word, the assembly exercises its priestly function by interceding for all humanity.

Priest's Introduction

The Priest calls the assembly to prayer.

Intentions

As a rule the series of intentions is:
  1 for the needs of the Church
  2 for public authorities and the salvation of the whole world
  3 for those burdened with any kind of difficulty
  4 for the local community

Nevertheless, in particular celebrations such as Confirmation, Marriage, or a Funeral, the series of intentions may reflect more closely the particular occasion.

The Deacon, or a Reader, announces short intentions for prayer to the assembly.

After each intention there is a significant pause while the assembly prays, then the response is sung or said.

Example responses:

Deacon or Reader: We pray to the Lord.
All: **Lord, hear our prayer.**

or

Deacon or Reader: Let us pray to the Lord,
All: **Grant this, almighty God.**

or

Deacon or Reader: Let us pray to the Lord,
All: **Christ, hear us.** *or* **Christ, graciously hear us.**

or

Deacon or Reader: Let us pray to the Lord,
All: **Lord, have mercy.** *or* **Kyrie, eleison.**

After the final intention and response, there may be a period of silent prayer.

Priest's Prayer

Then the Priest says a concluding prayer to which all reply:

All: **Amen.**

ALL SIT

LITURGY OF THE EUCHARIST

> *Their eyes were opened and they recognised him in the breaking of bread.*
> *(cf Luke 24:30–31)*
>
> At the Last Supper, Christ instituted the Sacrifice and Paschal meal that make the Sacrifice of the cross present in the Church. From the days of the Apostles the Church has celebrated that Sacrifice by carrying out what the Lord did and handed over to his disciples to do in his memory. Like him, the Church has taken bread and wine, given thanks to God over them, broken the bread, and shared the bread and cup of blessing as the Body and Blood of Christ (cf 1 Corinthians 10:16).
>
> *Celebrating the Mass n 174*

PREPARATION OF THE GIFTS

A hymn or song may be sung, or instrumental music played during the collection, the procession, and the presentation of the gifts. If there is no music, the Priest may speak the following words aloud and the people acclaim the response at the end of each prayer.

Priest: Blessed are you, Lord God of all creation,
for through your goodness we have received
the bread we offer you:
fruit of the earth and work of human hands,
it will become for us the bread of life.

People: **Blessed be God for ever.**

Priest: Blessed are you, Lord God of all creation,
for through your goodness we have received
the wine we offer you:
fruit of the vine and work of human hands,
it will become our spiritual drink.

People: **Blessed be God for ever.**

ALL STAND

The Priest completes additional personal preparatory rites, and the people rise as he says:

Priest: Pray, brethren (brothers and sisters),
that my sacrifice and yours
may be acceptable to God,
the almighty Father.

▷ *Music p 212*

People: **May the Lord accept the sacrifice at your hands**
for the praise and glory of his name,
for our good
and the good of all his holy Church.

PRAYER OVER THE OFFERINGS

▷ *Proper*

Then the Priest says the Prayer over the Offerings, at the end of which the people acclaim:

People: **Amen.**

EUCHARISTIC PRAYER

The Eucharistic Prayer, the centre and summit of the entire celebration, sums up what it means for the Church to celebrate the Eucharist. It is a memorial proclamation of praise and thanksgiving for God's work of salvation, a proclamation in which the Body and Blood of Christ are made present by the power of the Holy Spirit and the people are joined to Christ in offering his Sacrifice to the Father. The Eucharistic Prayer is proclaimed by the Priest celebrant in the name of Christ and on behalf of the whole assembly, which professes its faith and gives its assent through dialogue, acclamations, and the Amen. Since the Eucharistic Prayer is the summit of the Mass, it is appropriate for its solemn nature and importance to be enhanced by being sung.

Celebrating the Mass n 186

Eucharistic Prayers I to IV are the principal prayers and are for use throughout the liturgical year. Eucharistic Prayer IV has a fixed preface and so may only be used when a Mass has no preface of its own and on Sundays in Ordinary Time. Eucharistic Prayers I to IV and Eucharistic Prayers for Reconciliation I and II are printed in full, beginning on page 18.

PREFACE DIALOGUE

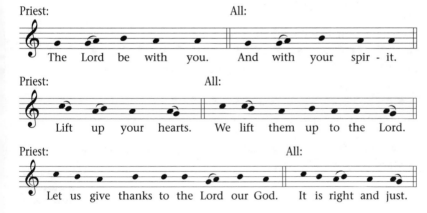

Priest: The Lord be with you. / All: And with your spirit.

Priest: Lift up your hearts. / All: We lift them up to the Lord.

Priest: Let us give thanks to the Lord our God. / All: It is right and just.

Priest: The Lord be with you.
People: **And with your spirit.**

Priest: Lift up your hearts.
People: **We lift them up to the Lord.**

Priest: Let us give thanks to the Lord our God.
People: **It is right and just.**

PREFACE

The Priest continues with the Preface.

SANCTUS

The Priest concludes the Preface with the people, singing or saying aloud:

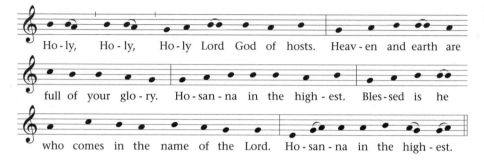

Ho-ly, Ho-ly, Ho-ly Lord God of hosts. Heav-en and earth are full of your glo-ry. Ho-san-na in the high-est. Bles-sed is he who comes in the name of the Lord. Ho-san-na in the high-est.

All: Holy, Holy, Holy Lord God of hosts.
          Heaven and earth are full of your glory.
          Hosanna in the highest.
          Blessed is he who comes in the name of the Lord.
          Hosanna in the highest.

or

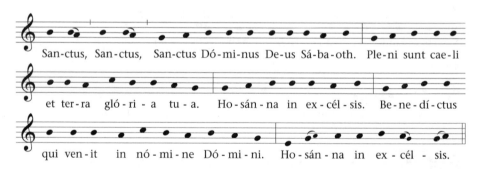

San-ctus, San-ctus, San-ctus Dó-mi-nus De-us Sá-ba-oth. Ple-ni sunt cae-li et ter-ra gló-ri-a tu-a. Ho-sán-na in ex-cél-sis. Be-ne-dí-ctus qui ven-it in nó-mi-ne Dó-mi-ni. Ho-sán-na in ex-cél-sis.

ALL KNEEL

Texts for Eucharistic Prayers I to IV, Eucharistic Prayers for Reconciliation I and II and Eucharistic Prayers for use in Masses for Various Needs I to IV follow on page 18.

MEMORIAL ACCLAMATION

The Memorial Acclamation follows the words of Institution and the elevation of the host and chalice.

The Priest sings:

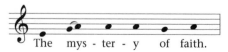

The mys-ter-y of faith.

And the people continue with one of the following acclamations.

Memorial Acclamation A

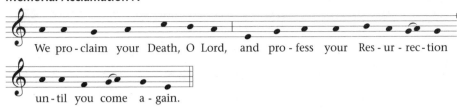

We pro - claim your Death, O Lord, and pro - fess your Res - ur - rec - tion

un - til you come a - gain.

Memorial Acclamation B

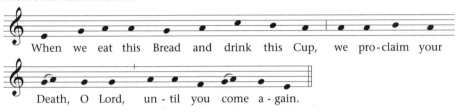

When we eat this Bread and drink this Cup, we pro - claim your

Death, O Lord, un - til you come a - gain.

Memorial Acclamation C

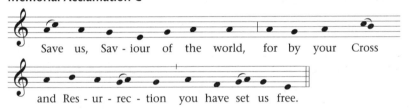

Save us, Sav - iour of the world, for by your Cross

and Res - ur - rec - tion you have set us free.

Memorial Acclamation D   *for Ireland only*

My Lord and my God.

Priest: The mystery of faith.
People: **We proclaim your Death, O Lord,**
      and profess your Resurrection
      until you come again.

or

People: **When we eat this Bread and drink this Cup,**
      we proclaim your Death, O Lord,
      until you come again.

or

People: **Save us, Saviour of the world,**
      for by your Cross and Resurrection
      you have set us free.

or for Ireland only:

People: **My Lord and my God.**

DOXOLOGY AND GREAT AMEN

At the end of the Eucharistic Prayer, the Priest takes the chalice and paten with the host and, raising both, he alone sings (or says) the Doxology. The people acclaim 'Amen'.

Priest:

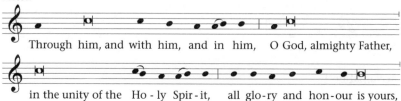

Through him, and with him, and in him,   O God, almighty Father,

in the unity of the Ho - ly Spir - it,   all glo-ry and hon-our is yours,

People:

for ev - er and   ev - er.   A - men.

Priest: Through him, and with him, and in him,
          O God, almighty Father,
          in the unity of the Holy Spirit,
          all glory and honour is yours,
          for ever and ever.
People: **Amen.**

▷ *page 56*

EUCHARISTIC PRAYERS

EUCHARISTIC PRAYER I

THE ROMAN CANON

On certain occasions, special forms of parts of the Eucharistic Prayer may be used.

Priest: To you, therefore, most merciful Father,
          we make humble prayer and petition
          through Jesus Christ, your Son, our Lord:
          that you accept
          and bless ✠ these gifts, these offerings,
          these holy and unblemished sacrifices,
          which we offer you firstly
          for your holy catholic Church.
          Be pleased to grant her peace,
          to guard, unite and govern her
          throughout the whole world,
          together with your servant N. our Pope
          and N. our Bishop,*
          and all those who, holding to the truth,
          hand on the catholic and apostolic faith.

---

* Mention may be made here of the Coadjutor Bishop, or Auxiliary Bishops

ORDER

Commemoration of the Living

Remember, Lord, your servants N. and N.
and all gathered here,
whose faith and devotion are known to you.
For them, we offer you this sacrifice of praise
or they offer it for themselves
and all who are dear to them:
for the redemption of their souls,
in hope of health and well-being,
and paying their homage to you,
the eternal God, living and true.

Communicantes

In communion with those whose memory we venerate,
especially the glorious ever-Virgin Mary,
Mother of our God and Lord, Jesus Christ,
and blessed Joseph, her Spouse,
your blessed Apostles and Martyrs,
Peter and Paul, Andrew,
(James, John,
Thomas, James, Philip,
Bartholomew, Matthew,
Simon and Jude;
Linus, Cletus, Clement, Sixtus,
Cornelius, Cyprian,
Lawrence, Chrysogonus,
John and Paul,
Cosmas and Damian)
and all your Saints;
we ask that through their merits and prayers,
in all things we may be defended
by your protecting help.
(Through Christ our Lord. Amen.)

Hanc Igitur

Therefore, Lord, we pray:
graciously accept this oblation of our service,
that of your whole family;
order our days in your peace,
and command that we be delivered from eternal damnation
and counted among the flock of those you have chosen.
(Through Christ our Lord. Amen.)

Be pleased, O God, we pray,
to bless, acknowledge,
and approve this offering in every respect;
make it spiritual and acceptable,
so that it may become for us
the Body and Blood of your most beloved Son,
our Lord Jesus Christ.

On the day before he was to suffer,
he took bread in his holy and venerable hands,
and with eyes raised to heaven
to you, O God, his almighty Father,
giving you thanks, he said the blessing,
broke the bread
and gave it to his disciples, saying:

TAKE THIS, ALL OF YOU, AND EAT OF IT,
FOR THIS IS MY BODY,
WHICH WILL BE GIVEN UP FOR YOU.

In a similar way, when supper was ended,
he took this precious chalice
in his holy and venerable hands,
and once more giving you thanks, he said the blessing
and gave the chalice to his disciples, saying:

TAKE THIS, ALL OF YOU, AND DRINK FROM IT,
FOR THIS IS THE CHALICE OF MY BLOOD,
THE BLOOD OF THE NEW AND ETERNAL COVENANT,
WHICH WILL BE POURED OUT FOR YOU AND FOR MANY
FOR THE FORGIVENESS OF SINS.

DO THIS IN MEMORY OF ME.

Memorial Acclamation

The Priest sings:

The   mys - ter - y   of   faith.

And the people continue with one of the following acclamations:

ORDER

Memorial Acclamation A

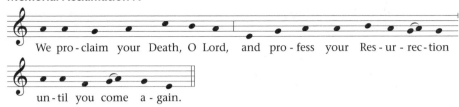

We pro-claim your Death, O Lord, and pro-fess your Res-ur-rec-tion un-til you come a-gain.

Memorial Acclamation B

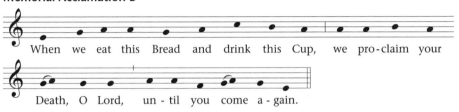

When we eat this Bread and drink this Cup, we pro-claim your Death, O Lord, un-til you come a-gain.

Memorial Acclamation C

Save us, Sav-iour of the world, for by your Cross and Res-ur-rec-tion you have set us free.

Memorial Acclamation D   *for Ireland only*

My Lord and my God.

Priest: Therefore, O Lord,
as we celebrate the memorial of the blessed Passion,
the Resurrection from the dead,
and the glorious Ascension into heaven
of Christ, your Son, our Lord,
we, your servants and your holy people,
offer to your glorious majesty
from the gifts that you have given us,
this pure victim,
this holy victim,
this spotless victim,
the holy Bread of eternal life
and the Chalice of everlasting salvation.

Be pleased to look upon these offerings
with a serene and kindly countenance,
and to accept them,
as once you were pleased to accept
the gifts of your servant Abel the just,
the sacrifice of Abraham, our father in faith,
and the offering of your high priest Melchizedek,
a holy sacrifice, a spotless victim.

In humble prayer we ask you, almighty God:
command that these gifts be borne
by the hands of your holy Angel
to your altar on high
in the sight of your divine majesty,
so that all of us, who through this participation at the altar
receive the most holy Body and Blood of your Son,
may be filled with every grace and heavenly blessing.
(Through Christ our Lord. Amen.)

Commemoration of the Dead
Remember also, Lord, your servants N. and N.,
who have gone before us with the sign of faith
and rest in the sleep of peace.
Grant them, O Lord, we pray,
and all who sleep in Christ,
a place of refreshment, light and peace.
(Through Christ our Lord. Amen.)

To us, also, your servants, who, though sinners,
hope in your abundant mercies,
graciously grant some share
and fellowship with your holy Apostles and Martyrs:
with John the Baptist, Stephen,
Matthias, Barnabas,
(Ignatius, Alexander,
Marcellinus, Peter,
Felicity, Perpetua,
Agatha, Lucy,
Agnes, Cecilia, Anastasia)
and all your Saints;
admit us, we beseech you,
into their company,
not weighing our merits,
but granting us your pardon,
through Christ our Lord.

Through whom
you continue to make all these good things, O Lord;
you sanctify them, fill them with life,
bless them, and bestow them upon us.

Doxology and Great Amen

At the end of the Eucharistic Prayer, the Priest takes the chalice and paten with the host and, raising both, he alone sings (or says) the Doxology. The people acclaim 'Amen'.

Priest: Through him, and with him, and in him,
               O God, almighty Father,
               in the unity of the Holy Spirit,
               all glory and honour is yours,
               for ever and ever.

People: **Amen.**

Priest: People:

...for   ev - er   and   ev - er.   A - men.

▷ *page 56*

EUCHARISTIC PRAYER II

This Eucharistic Prayer has its own Preface, but it may also be used with other Prefaces, especially those that present an overall view of the mystery of salvation.

On certain occasions, special forms of parts of the Eucharistic Prayer may be used.

Preface Dialogue

Priest: All:

The   Lord   be   with   you.   And   with   your   spir - it.

Priest: All:

Lift   up   your   hearts.   We   lift   them   up   to   the   Lord.

Priest: All:

Let   us   give   thanks   to   the   Lord   our   God.   It   is   right   and   just.

Preface

Priest: It is truly right and just, our duty and our salvation,
always and everywhere to give you thanks, Father most holy,
through your beloved Son, Jesus Christ,
your Word through whom you made all things,
whom you sent as our Saviour and Redeemer,
incarnate by the Holy Spirit and born of the Virgin.

Fulfilling your will and gaining for you a holy people,
he stretched out his hands as he endured his Passion,
so as to break the bonds of death and manifest the resurrection.

And so, with the Angels and all the Saints
we declare your glory,
as with one voice we acclaim:

Sanctus

All:

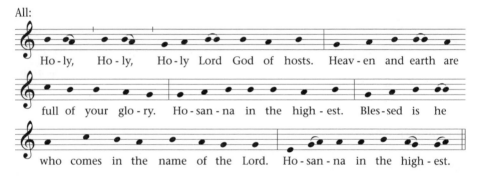

Ho-ly, Ho-ly, Ho-ly Lord God of hosts. Heav-en and earth are full of your glo-ry. Ho-san-na in the high-est. Bles-sed is he who comes in the name of the Lord. Ho-san-na in the high-est.

Priest: You are indeed Holy, O Lord,   **ALL KNEEL**
the fount of all holiness.
Make holy, therefore, these gifts, we pray,
by sending down your Spirit upon them like the dewfall,
so that they may become for us
the Body and ✠ Blood of our Lord Jesus Christ.

At the time he was betrayed
and entered willingly into his Passion,
he took bread and, giving thanks, broke it,
and gave it to his disciples, saying:

TAKE THIS, ALL OF YOU, AND EAT OF IT,
FOR THIS IS MY BODY,
WHICH WILL BE GIVEN UP FOR YOU.

In a similar way, when supper was ended,
he took the chalice
and, once more giving thanks,
he gave it to his disciples, saying:

TAKE THIS, ALL OF YOU, AND DRINK FROM IT,
FOR THIS IS THE CHALICE OF MY BLOOD,
THE BLOOD OF THE NEW AND ETERNAL COVENANT,
WHICH WILL BE POURED OUT FOR YOU AND FOR MANY
FOR THE FORGIVENESS OF SINS.

DO THIS IN MEMORY OF ME.

Memorial Acclamation

The Priest sings:

The mys - ter - y of faith.

And the people continue with one of the following acclamations:

Memorial Acclamation A

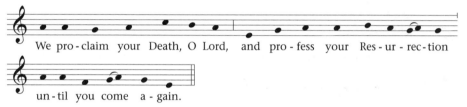

We pro - claim your Death, O Lord, and pro - fess your Res - ur - rec - tion un - til you come a - gain.

Memorial Acclamation B

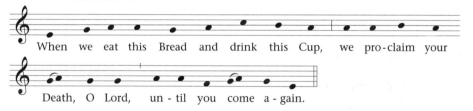

When we eat this Bread and drink this Cup, we pro - claim your Death, O Lord, un - til you come a - gain.

Memorial Acclamation C

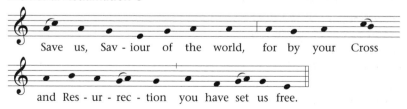

Save us, Sav - iour of the world, for by your Cross and Res - ur - rec - tion you have set us free.

Memorial Acclamation D   *for Ireland only*

My Lord and my God.

Priest: Therefore, as we celebrate
the memorial of his Death and Resurrection,
we offer you, Lord,
the Bread of life and the Chalice of salvation,
giving thanks that you have held us worthy
to be in your presence and minister to you.

Humbly we pray
that, partaking of the Body and Blood of Christ,
we may be gathered into one by the Holy Spirit.

Remember, Lord, your Church,
spread throughout the world,
and bring her to the fullness of charity,
together with N. our Pope and N. our Bishop *
and all the clergy.

In Masses for the Dead, the following may be added:
Remember your servant N.,
whom you have called (today)
from this world to yourself.
Grant that he (she) who was united with your Son in a death like his,
may also be one with him in his Resurrection.

Remember also our brothers and sisters
who have fallen asleep in the hope of the resurrection,
and all who have died in your mercy:
welcome them into the light of your face.
Have mercy on us all, we pray,
that with the Blessed Virgin Mary, Mother of God,
with blessed Joseph, her Spouse,
with the blessed Apostles,
and all the Saints who have pleased you throughout the ages,
we may merit to be coheirs to eternal life,
and may praise and glorify you
through your Son, Jesus Christ.

Doxology and Great Amen

At the end of the Eucharistic Prayer, the Priest takes the chalice and paten with the host and, raising both, he alone sings (or says) the Doxology. The people acclaim 'Amen'.

Priest: Through him, and with him, and in him,
          O God, almighty Father,
          in the unity of the Holy Spirit,
          all glory and honour is yours,
          for ever and ever.

People: **Amen.**

Priest: People:

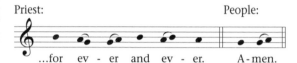

...for   ev - er   and   ev - er.   A - men.

▷ *page 56*

EUCHARISTIC PRAYER III

On certain occasions, special forms of parts of the Eucharistic Prayer may be used.

Priest: You are indeed Holy, O Lord,
          and all you have created
          rightly gives you praise,
          for through your Son our Lord Jesus Christ,
          by the power and working of the Holy Spirit,
          you give life to all things and make them holy,
          and you never cease to gather a people to yourself,
          so that from the rising of the sun to its setting
          a pure sacrifice may be offered to your name.

          Therefore, O Lord, we humbly implore you:
          by the same Spirit graciously make holy
          these gifts we have brought to you for consecration,
          that they may become the Body and ✠ Blood
          of your Son our Lord Jesus Christ,
          at whose command we celebrate these mysteries.

          For on the night he was betrayed
          he himself took bread,
          and, giving you thanks, he said the blessing,
          broke the bread and gave it to his disciples, saying:

          TAKE THIS, ALL OF YOU, AND EAT OF IT,
          FOR THIS IS MY BODY,
          WHICH WILL BE GIVEN UP FOR YOU.

In a similar way, when supper was ended,
he took the chalice,
and, giving you thanks, he said the blessing,
and gave the chalice to his disciples, saying:

TAKE THIS, ALL OF YOU, AND DRINK FROM IT,
FOR THIS IS THE CHALICE OF MY BLOOD,
THE BLOOD OF THE NEW AND ETERNAL COVENANT,
WHICH WILL BE POURED OUT FOR YOU AND FOR MANY
FOR THE FORGIVENESS OF SINS.

DO THIS IN MEMORY OF ME.

Memorial Acclamation

The Priest sings:

The mys - ter - y of faith.

And the people continue with one of the following acclamations:

Memorial Acclamation A

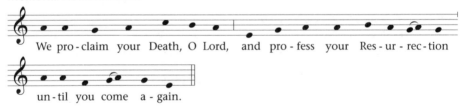

We pro - claim your Death, O Lord, and pro - fess your Res - ur - rec - tion

un - til you come a - gain.

Memorial Acclamation B

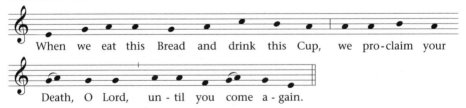

When we eat this Bread and drink this Cup, we pro - claim your

Death, O Lord, un - til you come a - gain.

Memorial Acclamation C

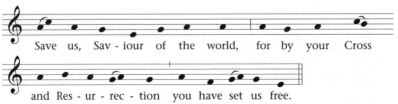

Save us, Sav - iour of the world, for by your Cross

and Res - ur - rec - tion you have set us free.

Memorial Acclamation D   *for Ireland only*

My   Lord   and   my   God.

ORDER

Priest: Therefore, O Lord, as we celebrate the memorial
of the saving Passion of your Son,
his wondrous Resurrection
and Ascension into heaven,
and as we look forward to his second coming,
we offer you in thanksgiving
this holy and living sacrifice.

Look, we pray, upon the oblation of your Church
and, recognizing the sacrificial Victim by whose death
you willed to reconcile us to yourself,
grant that we, who are nourished
by the Body and Blood of your Son
and filled with his Holy Spirit,
may become one body, one spirit in Christ.

May he make of us
an eternal offering to you,
so that we may obtain an inheritance with your elect,
especially with the most Blessed Virgin Mary, Mother of God,
with blessed Joseph, her Spouse,
with your blessed Apostles and glorious Martyrs
(with Saint N.: *the Saint of the day or Patron Saint*)
and with all the Saints,
on whose constant intercession in your presence
we rely for unfailing help.

May this Sacrifice of our reconciliation,
we pray, O Lord,
advance the peace and salvation of all the world.
Be pleased to confirm in faith and charity
your pilgrim Church on earth,
with your servant N. our Pope and N. our Bishop,*
the Order of Bishops, all the clergy,
and the entire people you have gained for your own.

Listen graciously to the prayers of this family,
whom you have summoned before you:
in your compassion, O merciful Father,
gather to yourself all your children
scattered throughout the world.

---

* Mention may be made here of the Coadjutor Bishop, or Auxiliary Bishops

† To our departed brothers and sisters
and to all who were pleasing to you
at their passing from this life,
give kind admittance to your kingdom.
There we hope to enjoy for ever the fullness of your glory
through Christ our Lord,
through whom you bestow on the world all that is good. †

In Masses for the Dead, the following may be said:
† Remember your servant N.
whom you have called (today)
from this world to yourself.
Grant that he (she) who was united with your Son in a death like his,
may also be one with him in his Resurrection,
when from the earth
he will raise up in the flesh those who have died,
and transform our lowly body
after the pattern of his own glorious body.
To our departed brothers and sisters, too,
and to all who were pleasing to you
at their passing from this life,
give kind admittance to your kingdom.
There we hope to enjoy for ever the fullness of your glory,
when you will wipe away every tear from our eyes.
For seeing you, our God, as you are,
we shall be like you for all the ages
and praise you without end,
through Christ our Lord,
through whom you bestow on the world all that is good. †

Doxology and Great Amen

At the end of the Eucharistic Prayer, the Priest takes the chalice and paten with the host and, raising both, he alone sings (or says) the Doxology. The people acclaim 'Amen'.

Priest: Through him, and with him, and in him,
           O God, almighty Father,
           in the unity of the Holy Spirit,
           all glory and honour is yours,
           for ever and ever.
People: **Amen.**

Priest: People:

...for ev - er and ev - er.   A - men.

▷ *page 56*

EUCHARISTIC PRAYER IV

This Eucharistic Prayer has its own Preface which may not be replaced by another, because of the structure of the Prayer itself, which presents a summary of the history of salvation.
On certain occasions, special forms of parts of the Eucharistic Prayer may be used.

Preface Dialogue

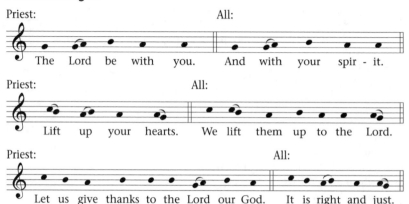

Priest: All:

The Lord be with you. And with your spir - it.

Priest: All:

Lift up your hearts. We lift them up to the Lord.

Priest: All:

Let us give thanks to the Lord our God. It is right and just.

Preface

Priest: It is truly right to give you thanks,
truly just to give you glory, Father most holy,
for you are the one God living and true,
existing before all ages and abiding for all eternity,
dwelling in unapproachable light;
yet you, who alone are good, the source of life,
have made all that is,
so that you might fill your creatures with blessings
and bring joy to many of them by the glory of your light.

And so, in your presence are countless hosts of Angels,
who serve you day and night
and, gazing upon the glory of your face,
glorify you without ceasing.

With them we, too, confess your name in exultation,
giving voice to every creature under heaven,
as we acclaim:

Sanctus *(see over)*

Sanctus

All:

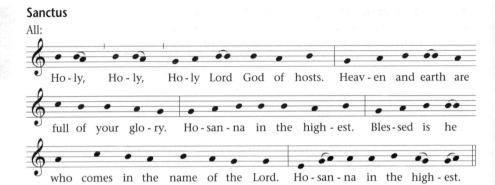

Ho-ly, Ho-ly, Ho-ly Lord God of hosts. Heav-en and earth are full of your glo-ry. Ho-san-na in the high-est. Bles-sed is he who comes in the name of the Lord. Ho-san-na in the high-est.

ALL KNEEL

Priest: We give you praise, Father most holy,
for you are great
and you have fashioned all your works
in wisdom and in love.
You formed man in your own image
and entrusted the whole world to his care,
so that in serving you alone, the Creator,
he might have dominion over all creatures.
And when through disobedience he had lost your friendship,
you did not abandon him to the domain of death.
For you came in mercy to the aid of all,
so that those who seek might find you.
Time and again you offered them covenants
and through the prophets
taught them to look forward to salvation.

And you so loved the world, Father most holy,
that in the fullness of time
you sent your Only Begotten Son to be our Saviour.
Made incarnate by the Holy Spirit
and born of the Virgin Mary,
he shared our human nature
in all things but sin.
To the poor he proclaimed the good news of salvation,
to prisoners, freedom,
and to the sorrowful of heart, joy.
To accomplish your plan,
he gave himself up to death,
and, rising from the dead,
he destroyed death and restored life.

And that we might live no longer for ourselves
but for him who died and rose again for us,
he sent the Holy Spirit from you, Father,
as the first fruits for those who believe,
so that, bringing to perfection his work in the world,
he might sanctify creation to the full.

Therefore, O Lord, we pray:
may this same Holy Spirit
graciously sanctify these offerings,
that they may become
the Body and ✠ Blood of our Lord Jesus Christ
for the celebration of this great mystery,
which he himself left us
as an eternal covenant.

For when the hour had come
for him to be glorified by you, Father most holy,
having loved his own who were in the world,
he loved them to the end:
and while they were at supper,
he took bread, blessed and broke it,
and gave it to his disciples, saying:

TAKE THIS, ALL OF YOU, AND EAT OF IT,
FOR THIS IS MY BODY,
WHICH WILL BE GIVEN UP FOR YOU.

In a similar way,
taking the chalice filled with the fruit of the vine,
he gave thanks,
and gave the chalice to his disciples, saying:

TAKE THIS, ALL OF YOU, AND DRINK FROM IT,
FOR THIS IS THE CHALICE OF MY BLOOD,
THE BLOOD OF THE NEW AND ETERNAL COVENANT,
WHICH WILL BE POURED OUT FOR YOU AND FOR MANY
FOR THE FORGIVENESS OF SINS.

DO THIS IN MEMORY OF ME.

Memorial Acclamation

The Priest sings:

The mys - ter - y of faith.

And the people continue with one of the following acclamations:

Memorial Acclamation A

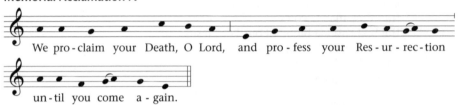

We pro - claim your Death, O Lord, and pro - fess your Res - ur - rec - tion

un - til you come a - gain.

Memorial Acclamation B

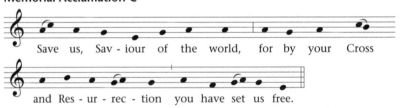

When we eat this Bread and drink this Cup, we pro - claim your

Death, O Lord, un - til you come a - gain.

Memorial Acclamation C

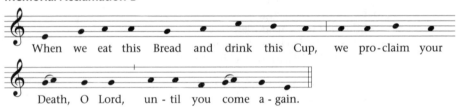

Save us, Sav - iour of the world, for by your Cross

and Res - ur - rec - tion you have set us free.

Memorial Acclamation D *for Ireland only*

My Lord and my God.

ORDER

Priest: Therefore, O Lord,
as we now celebrate the memorial of our redemption,
we remember Christ's Death
and his descent to the realm of the dead,
we proclaim his Resurrection
and his Ascension to your right hand,
and as we await his coming in glory,
we offer you his Body and Blood,
the sacrifice acceptable to you
which brings salvation to the whole world.

Look, O Lord, upon the Sacrifice
which you yourself have provided for your Church,
and grant in your loving kindness
to all who partake of this one Bread and one Chalice
that, gathered into one body by the Holy Spirit,
they may truly become a living sacrifice in Christ
to the praise of your glory.

Therefore, Lord, remember now
all for whom we offer this sacrifice:
especially your servant N. our Pope,
N. our Bishop,* and the whole Order of Bishops,
all the clergy,
those who take part in this offering,
those gathered here before you,
your entire people,
and all who seek you with a sincere heart.

Remember also
those who have died in the peace of your Christ
and all the dead,
whose faith you alone have known.

To all of us, your children,
grant, O merciful Father,
that we may enter into a heavenly inheritance
with the Blessed Virgin Mary, Mother of God,
with blessed Joseph, her Spouse,
and with your Apostles and Saints in your kingdom.
There, with the whole of creation,
freed from the corruption of sin and death,
may we glorify you through Christ our Lord,
through whom you bestow on the world all that is good.

---

* Mention may be made here of the Coadjutor Bishop, or Auxiliary Bishops

Doxology and Great Amen

At the end of the Eucharistic Prayer, the Priest takes the chalice and paten with the host and, raising both, he alone sings (or says) the Doxology. The people acclaim 'Amen'.

Priest: Through him, and with him, and in him,
             O God, almighty Father,
             in the unity of the Holy Spirit,
             all glory and honour is yours,
             for ever and ever.

People: **Amen.**

Priest: People:

   ...for ev - er and ev - er.   A - men.

▷ *page 56*

EUCHARISTIC PRAYER FOR RECONCILIATION I

The Eucharistic Prayers for Reconciliation may be used in Masses in which the mystery of reconciliation is conveyed to the faithful in a special way, including Masses during Lent.

Although these Eucharistic Prayers have been provided with a proper Preface, they may also be used with other Prefaces that refer to penance and conversion, as, for example, the Prefaces of Lent.

Priest: The Lord be with you.   ▷ *Music p 15*
People: **And with your spirit.**

Priest: Lift up your hearts.
People: **We lift them up to the Lord.**

Priest: Let us give thanks to the Lord our God.
People: **It is right and just.**

Priest: It is truly right and just
             that we should always give you thanks,
             Lord, holy Father, almighty and eternal God.

             For you do not cease to spur us on
             to possess a more abundant life
             and, being rich in mercy,
             you constantly offer pardon
             and call on sinners
             to trust in your forgiveness alone.

             Never did you turn away from us,
             and, though time and again we have broken your covenant,
             you have bound the human family to yourself
             through Jesus your Son, our Redeemer,
             with a new bond of love so tight
             that it can never be undone.

Even now you set before your people
a time of grace and reconciliation,
and, as they turn back to you in spirit,
you grant them hope in Christ Jesus
and a desire to be of service to all,
while they entrust themselves
more fully to the Holy Spirit.

And so, filled with wonder,
we extol the power of your love,
and, proclaiming our joy
at the salvation that comes from you,
we join in the heavenly hymn of countless hosts,
as without end we acclaim:

All: **Holy, Holy, Holy Lord God of hosts.**   ▷ *Music p 16*
Heaven and earth are full of your glory.
Hosanna in the highest.
Blessed is he who comes in the name of the Lord.
Hosanna in the highest.

Priest: You are indeed Holy, O Lord,   **ALL KNEEL**
and from the world's beginning
are ceaselessly at work,
so that the human race may become holy,
just as you yourself are holy.

Look, we pray, upon your people's offerings
and pour out on them the power of your Spirit,
that they may become the Body and ✠ Blood
of your beloved Son, Jesus Christ,
in whom we, too, are your sons and daughters.

Indeed, though we once were lost
and could not approach you,
you loved us with the greatest love:
for your Son, who alone is just,
handed himself over to death,
and did not disdain to be nailed for our sake
to the wood of the Cross.

But before his arms were outstretched between heaven and earth,
to become the lasting sign of your covenant,
he desired to celebrate the Passover with his disciples.

As he ate with them,
he took bread
and, giving you thanks, he said the blessing,
broke the bread and gave it to them, saying:

TAKE THIS, ALL OF YOU, AND EAT OF IT,
FOR THIS IS MY BODY,
WHICH WILL BE GIVEN UP FOR YOU.

In a similar way, when supper was ended,
knowing that he was about to reconcile all things in himself
through his Blood to be shed on the Cross,
he took the chalice, filled with the fruit of the vine,
and once more giving you thanks,
handed the chalice to his disciples, saying:

TAKE THIS, ALL OF YOU, AND DRINK FROM IT,
FOR THIS IS THE CHALICE OF MY BLOOD,
THE BLOOD OF THE NEW AND ETERNAL COVENANT,
WHICH WILL BE POURED OUT FOR YOU AND FOR MANY
FOR THE FORGIVENESS OF SINS.

DO THIS IN MEMORY OF ME.

Priest: The mystery of faith.   ▷ Music p 17
People: **We proclaim your Death, O Lord,**
           and profess your Resurrection
           until you come again.
or
People: **When we eat this Bread and drink this Cup,**
           we proclaim your Death, O Lord,
           until you come again.
or
People: **Save us, Saviour of the world,**
           for by your Cross and Resurrection
           you have set us free.

or for Ireland only:
People: **My Lord and my God.**

Priest: Therefore, as we celebrate
           the memorial of your Son Jesus Christ,
           who is our Passover and our surest peace,
           we celebrate his Death and Resurrection from the dead,
           and looking forward to his blessed Coming,
           we offer you, who are our faithful and merciful God,
           this sacrificial Victim
           who reconciles to you the human race.

           Look kindly, most compassionate Father,
           on those you unite to yourself
           by the Sacrifice of your Son,
           and grant that, by the power of the Holy Spirit,
           as they partake of this one Bread and one Chalice,

they may be gathered into one Body in Christ,
who heals every division.

Be pleased to keep us always
in communion of mind and heart,
together with N. our Pope and N. our Bishop.*
Help us to work together
for the coming of your Kingdom,
until the hour when we stand before you,
Saints among the Saints in the halls of heaven,
with the Blessed Virgin Mary, Mother of God,
the blessed Apostles and all the Saints,
and with our deceased brothers and sisters,
whom we humbly commend to your mercy.

Then, freed at last from the wound of corruption
and made fully into a new creation,
we shall sing to you with gladness
the thanksgiving of Christ,
who lives for all eternity.

Priest: Through him, and with him, and in him,   ▷ Music p 18
          O God, almighty Father,
          in the unity of the Holy Spirit,
          all glory and honour is yours,
          for ever and ever.

People: **Amen.**

▷ page 56

EUCHARISTIC PRAYER FOR RECONCILIATION II

The Eucharistic Prayers for Reconciliation may be used in Masses in which the mystery of reconciliation is conveyed to the faithful in a special way, including Masses during Lent.

Although these Eucharistic Prayers have been provided with a proper Preface, they may also be used with other Prefaces that refer to penance and conversion, as, for example, the Prefaces of Lent.

Preface
Priest: The Lord be with you.   ▷ Music p 15
People: **And with your spirit.**

Priest: Lift up your hearts.
People: **We lift them up to the Lord.**

Priest: Let us give thanks to the Lord our God.
People: **It is right and just.**

Priest: It is truly right and just
          that we should give you thanks and praise,
          O God, almighty Father,

---

* Mention may be made here of the Coadjutor Bishop, or Auxiliary Bishops

for all you do in this world,
through our Lord Jesus Christ.

For though the human race
is divided by dissension and discord,
yet we know that by testing us
you change our hearts
to prepare them for reconciliation.

Even more, by your Spirit you move human hearts
that enemies may speak to each other again,
adversaries may join hands,
and peoples seek to meet together.

By the working of your power
it comes about, O Lord,
that hatred is overcome by love,
revenge gives way to forgiveness,
and discord is changed to mutual respect.

Therefore, as we give you ceaseless thanks
with the choirs of heaven,
we cry out to your majesty on earth,
and without end we acclaim:

All: **Holy, Holy, Holy Lord God of hosts.**   ▷ *Music p 16*
          Heaven and earth are full of your glory.
          Hosanna in the highest.
          Blessed is he who comes in the name of the Lord.
          Hosanna in the highest.

ALL KNEEL

Priest: You, therefore, almighty Father,
          we bless through Jesus Christ your Son,
          who comes in your name.
          He himself is the Word that brings salvation,
          the hand you extend to sinners,
          the way by which your peace is offered to us.
          When we ourselves had turned away from you
          on account of our sins,
          you brought us back to be reconciled, O Lord,
          so that, converted at last to you,
          we might love one another
          through your Son,
          whom for our sake you handed over to death.

          And now, celebrating the reconciliation
          Christ has brought us,
          we entreat you:
          sanctify these gifts by the outpouring of your Spirit,

ORDER

that they may become the Body and ✠ Blood of your Son,
whose command we fulfil
when we celebrate these mysteries.

For when about to give his life to set us free,
as he reclined at supper,
he himself took bread into his hands,
and, giving you thanks, he said the blessing,
broke the bread and gave it to his disciples, saying:

TAKE THIS, ALL OF YOU, AND EAT OF IT,
FOR THIS IS MY BODY,
WHICH WILL BE GIVEN UP FOR YOU.

In a similar way, on that same evening,
he took the chalice of blessing in his hands,
confessing your mercy,
and gave the chalice to his disciples, saying:

TAKE THIS, ALL OF YOU, AND DRINK FROM IT,
FOR THIS IS THE CHALICE OF MY BLOOD,
THE BLOOD OF THE NEW AND ETERNAL COVENANT,
WHICH WILL BE POURED OUT FOR YOU AND FOR MANY
FOR THE FORGIVENESS OF SINS.

DO THIS IN MEMORY OF ME.

Priest: The mystery of faith.   ▷ Music p 17
People: **We proclaim your Death, O Lord,**
           and profess your Resurrection
           until you come again.
or
People: **When we eat this Bread and drink this Cup,**
           we proclaim your Death, O Lord,
           until you come again.
or
People: **Save us, Saviour of the world,**
           for by your Cross and Resurrection
           you have set us free.

or for Ireland only:
People: **My Lord and my God.**

Priest: Celebrating, therefore, the memorial
           of the Death and Resurrection of your Son,
           who left us this pledge of his love,
           we offer you what you have bestowed on us,
           the Sacrifice of perfect reconciliation.

Holy Father, we humbly beseech you
to accept us also, together with your Son,
and in this saving banquet
graciously to endow us with his very Spirit,
who takes away everything
that estranges us from one another.

May he make your Church a sign of unity
and an instrument of your peace among all people
and may he keep us in communion
with N. our Pope and N. our Bishop *
and all the Bishops
and your entire people.

Just as you have gathered us now at the table of your Son,
so also bring us together,
with the glorious Virgin Mary, Mother of God,
with your blessed Apostles and all the Saints,
with our brothers and sisters
and those of every race and tongue
who have died in your friendship.
Bring us to share with them the unending banquet of unity
in a new heaven and a new earth,
where the fullness of your peace will shine forth
in Christ Jesus our Lord.

Priest:	Through him, and with him, and in him,
	O God, almighty Father,
	in the unity of the Holy Spirit,
	all glory and honour is yours,
	for ever and ever.
People:	**Amen.**

▷ Music p 18

▷ page 56

---

* Mention may be made here of the Coadjutor Bishop, or Auxiliary Bishops

EUCHARISTIC PRAYERS FOR USE IN MASSES FOR VARIOUS NEEDS

These Eucharistic Prayers have their own Prefaces which may not be replaced by another, because of the structure of the Prayers themselves.

I THE CHURCH ON THE PATH OF UNITY

Priest: The Lord be with you.   ▷ *Music p 15*
People: **And with your spirit.**

Priest: Lift up your hearts.
People: **We lift them up to the Lord.**

Priest: Let us give thanks to the Lord our God.
People: **It is right and just.**

Priest: It is truly right and just to give you thanks
and raise to you a hymn of glory and praise,
O Lord, Father of infinite goodness.

For by the word of your Son's Gospel
you have brought together one Church
from every people, tongue, and nation,
and, having filled her with life by the power of your Spirit,
you never cease through her
to gather the whole human race into one.

Manifesting the covenant of your love,
she dispenses without ceasing
the blessed hope of your Kingdom
and shines bright as the sign of your faithfulness,
which in Christ Jesus our Lord
you promised would last for eternity.

And so, with all the Powers of heaven,
we worship you constantly on earth,
while, with all the Church,
as one voice we acclaim:

All: **Holy, Holy, Holy Lord God of hosts.**   ▷ *Music p 16*
Heaven and earth are full of your glory.
Hosanna in the highest.
Blessed is he who comes in the name of the Lord.
Hosanna in the highest.

You are indeed Holy and to be glorified, O God,
who love the human race
and who always walk with us on the journey of life.
Blessed indeed is your Son,
present in our midst
when we are gathered by his love,
and when, as once for the disciples, so now for us,
he opens the Scriptures and breaks the bread.

Therefore, Father most merciful,
we ask that you send forth your Holy Spirit
to sanctify these gifts of bread and wine,
that they may become for us
the Body and ✠ Blood
of our Lord Jesus Christ.

On the day before he was to suffer,
on the night of the Last Supper,
he took bread and said the blessing,
broke the bread and gave it to his disciples, saying:

TAKE THIS, ALL OF YOU, AND EAT OF IT,
FOR THIS IS MY BODY,
WHICH WILL BE GIVEN UP FOR YOU.

In a similar way, when supper was ended,
he took the chalice, gave you thanks
and gave the chalice to his disciples, saying:

TAKE THIS, ALL OF YOU, AND DRINK FROM IT,
FOR THIS IS THE CHALICE OF MY BLOOD,
THE BLOOD OF THE NEW AND ETERNAL COVENANT,
WHICH WILL BE POURED OUT FOR YOU AND FOR MANY
FOR THE FORGIVENESS OF SINS.

DO THIS IN MEMORY OF ME.

Priest: The mystery of faith.   ▷ *Music p 17*
People: **We proclaim your Death, O Lord,**
and profess your Resurrection
until you come again.

or

People: **When we eat this Bread and drink this Cup,**
we proclaim your Death, O Lord,
until you come again.

or

People: **Save us, Saviour of the world,**
for by your Cross and Resurrection
you have set us free.

or   *for Ireland only:*

People: **My Lord and my God.**

Therefore, holy Father,
as we celebrate the memorial of Christ your Son, our Saviour,
whom you led through his Passion and Death on the Cross
to the glory of the Resurrection,
and whom you have seated at your right hand,
we proclaim the work of your love until he comes again
and we offer you the Bread of life
and the Chalice of blessing.

Look with favour on the oblation of your Church,
in which we show forth
the paschal Sacrifice of Christ that has been handed on to us,
and grant that, by the power of the Spirit of your love,
we may be counted now and until the day of eternity
among the members of your Son,
in whose Body and Blood we have communion.

Lord, renew your Church (which is in N.)
by the light of the Gospel.
Strengthen the bond of unity
between the faithful and the pastors of your people,
together with N. our Pope, N. our Bishop,*
and the whole Order of Bishops,
that in a world torn by strife
your people may shine forth
as a prophetic sign of unity and concord.

Remember our brothers and sisters (N. and N.),
who have fallen asleep in the peace of your Christ,
and all the dead, whose faith you alone have known.
Admit them to rejoice in the light of your face,
and in the resurrection give them the fullness of life.

Grant also to us,
when our earthly pilgrimage is done,
that we may come to an eternal dwelling place
and live with you for ever;
there, in communion with the Blessed Virgin Mary, Mother of God,
with the Apostles and Martyrs,
(with Saint N.: *the Saint of the day or Patron*)
and with all the Saints,
we shall praise and exalt you
through Jesus Christ, your Son.

---

* Mention may be made here of the Coadjutor Bishop, or Auxiliary Bishops

Priest: Through him, and with him, and in him,   ▷ Music p 18
            O God, almighty Father,
            in the unity of the Holy Spirit,
            all glory and honour is yours,
            for ever and ever.

People: **Amen.**

▷ page 56

II   GOD GUIDES HIS CHURCH ALONG THE WAY OF SALVATION

Priest: The Lord be with you.   ▷ Music p 15
People: **And with your spirit.**

Priest: Lift up your hearts.
People: **We lift them up to the Lord.**

Priest: Let us give thanks to the Lord our God.
People: **It is right and just.**

            It is truly right and just, our duty and our salvation,
            always and everywhere to give you thanks,
            Lord, holy Father,
            creator of the world and source of all life.

            For you never forsake the works of your wisdom,
            but by your providence are even now at work in our midst.
            With mighty hand and outstretched arm
            you led your people Israel through the desert.
            Now, as your Church makes her pilgrim journey in the world,
            you always accompany her
            by the power of the Holy Spirit
            and lead her along the paths of time
            to the eternal joy of your Kingdom,
            through Christ our Lord.

            And so, with the Angels and Saints,
            we, too, sing the hymn of your glory,
            as without end we acclaim:

All: **Holy, Holy, Holy Lord God of hosts.**   ▷ Music p 16
            Heaven and earth are full of your glory.
            Hosanna in the highest.
            Blessed is he who comes in the name of the Lord.
            Hosanna in the highest.

Priest: You are indeed Holy and to be glorified, O God,
            who love the human race
            and who always walk with us on the journey of life.

Blessed indeed is your Son,
present in our midst
when we are gathered by his love
and when, as once for the disciples, so now for us,
he opens the Scriptures and breaks the bread.

Therefore, Father most merciful,
we ask that you send forth your Holy Spirit
to sanctify these gifts of bread and wine,
that they may become for us
the Body and ✠ Blood
of our Lord Jesus Christ.

On the day before he was to suffer,
on the night of the Last Supper,
he took bread and said the blessing,
broke the bread and gave it to his disciples, saying:

TAKE THIS, ALL OF YOU, AND EAT OF IT,
FOR THIS IS MY BODY,
WHICH WILL BE GIVEN UP FOR YOU.

In a similar way, when supper was ended,
he took the chalice, gave you thanks
and gave the chalice to his disciples, saying:

TAKE THIS, ALL OF YOU, AND DRINK FROM IT,
FOR THIS IS THE CHALICE OF MY BLOOD,
THE BLOOD OF THE NEW AND ETERNAL COVENANT,
WHICH WILL BE POURED OUT FOR YOU AND FOR MANY
FOR THE FORGIVENESS OF SINS.

DO THIS IN MEMORY OF ME.

Priest: The mystery of faith.   ▷ Music p 17
People: **We proclaim your Death, O Lord,**
and profess your Resurrection
until you come again.

or

People: **When we eat this Bread and drink this Cup,**
we proclaim your Death, O Lord,
until you come again.

or

People: **Save us, Saviour of the world,**
for by your Cross and Resurrection
you have set us free.

or   *for Ireland only:*

People: **My Lord and my God.**

Priest: Therefore, holy Father,
as we celebrate the memorial of Christ your Son, our Saviour,
whom you led through his Passion and Death on the Cross
to the glory of the Resurrection,
and whom you have seated at your right hand,
we proclaim the work of your love until he comes again
and we offer you the Bread of life
and the Chalice of blessing.

Look with favour on the oblation of your Church,
in which we show forth
the paschal Sacrifice of Christ that has been handed on to us,
and grant that, by the power of the Spirit of your love,
we may be counted now and until the day of eternity
among the members of your Son,
in whose Body and Blood we have communion.

And so, having called us to your table, Lord,
confirm us in unity,
so that, together with N. our Pope and N. our Bishop,*
with all Bishops, Priests and Deacons,
and your entire people,
as we walk your ways with faith and hope,
we may strive to bring joy and trust into the world.

Remember our brothers and sisters (N. and N.),
who have fallen asleep in the peace of your Christ,
and all the dead, whose faith you alone have known.
Admit them to rejoice in the light of your face,
and in the resurrection give them the fullness of life.

Grant also to us,
when our earthly pilgrimage is done,
that we may come to an eternal dwelling place
and live with you for ever;
there, in communion with the Blessed Virgin Mary, Mother of God,
with the Apostles and Martyrs,
(with Saint N.: the Saint of the day or Patron)
and with all the Saints,
we shall praise and exalt you
through Jesus Christ, your Son.

---

* Mention may be made here of the Coadjutor Bishop, or Auxiliary Bishops

Priest: Through him, and with him, and in him,   ▷ *Music p 18*
O God, almighty Father,
in the unity of the Holy Spirit,
all glory and honour is yours,
for ever and ever.

People: **Amen.**   ▷ *page 56*

III JESUS, THE WAY TO THE FATHER

Priest: The Lord be with you.   ▷ *Music p 15*
People: **And with your spirit.**

Priest: Lift up your hearts.
People: **We lift them up to the Lord.**

Priest: Let us give thanks to the Lord our God.
People: **It is right and just.**

Priest: It is truly right and just, our duty and our salvation,
always and everywhere to give you thanks,
holy Father, Lord of heaven and earth,
through Christ our Lord.

For by your Word you created the world
and you govern all things in harmony.
You gave us the same Word made flesh as Mediator,
and he has spoken your words to us
and called us to follow him.
He is the way that leads us to you,
the truth that sets us free,
the life that fills us with gladness.

Through your Son
you gather men and women,
whom you made for the glory of your name,
into one family,
redeemed by the Blood of his Cross
and signed with the seal of the Spirit.

Therefore, now and for ages unending,
with all the Angels,
we proclaim your glory,
as in joyful celebration we acclaim:

All: **Holy, Holy, Holy Lord God of hosts.**   ▷ *Music p 16*
Heaven and earth are full of your glory.
Hosanna in the highest.
Blessed is he who comes in the name of the Lord.
Hosanna in the highest.

Priest: You are indeed Holy and to be glorified, O God,
who love the human race
and who always walk with us on the journey of life.
Blessed indeed is your Son,
present in our midst
when we are gathered by his love
and when, as once for the disciples, so now for us,
he opens the Scriptures and breaks the bread.

Therefore, Father most merciful,
we ask that you send forth your Holy Spirit
to sanctify these gifts of bread and wine,
that they may become for us
the Body and ✠ Blood
of our Lord Jesus Christ.

On the day before he was to suffer,
on the night of the Last Supper,
he took bread and said the blessing,
broke the bread and gave it to his disciples, saying:

TAKE THIS, ALL OF YOU, AND EAT OF IT,
FOR THIS IS MY BODY,
WHICH WILL BE GIVEN UP FOR YOU.

In a similar way, when supper was ended,
he took the chalice, gave you thanks
and gave the chalice to his disciples, saying:

TAKE THIS, ALL OF YOU, AND DRINK FROM IT,
FOR THIS IS THE CHALICE OF MY BLOOD,
THE BLOOD OF THE NEW AND ETERNAL COVENANT,
WHICH WILL BE POURED OUT FOR YOU AND FOR MANY
FOR THE FORGIVENESS OF SINS.

DO THIS IN MEMORY OF ME.

Priest: The mystery of faith.   ▷ Music p 17
People: **We proclaim your Death, O Lord,
and profess your Resurrection
until you come again.**

or

People: **When we eat this Bread and drink this Cup,
we proclaim your Death, O Lord,
until you come again.**

or

People: **Save us, Saviour of the world,
for by your Cross and Resurrection
you have set us free.**

Or   *for Ireland only:*

People: **My Lord and my God.**

Priest: Therefore, holy Father,
as we celebrate the memorial of Christ your Son, our Saviour,
whom you led through his Passion and Death on the Cross
to the glory of the Resurrection,
and whom you have seated at your right hand,
we proclaim the work of your love until he comes again
and we offer you the Bread of life
and the Chalice of blessing.

Look with favour on the oblation of your Church,
in which we show forth
the paschal Sacrifice of Christ that has been handed on to us,
and grant that, by the power of the Spirit of your love,
we may be counted now and until the day of eternity
among the members of your Son,
in whose Body and Blood we have communion.

By our partaking of this mystery, almighty Father,
give us life through your Spirit,
grant that we may be conformed to the image of your Son,
and confirm us in the bond of communion,
together with N. our Pope and N. our Bishop,*
with all other Bishops,
with Priests and Deacons,
and with your entire people.

Grant that all the faithful of the Church,
looking into the signs of the times by the light of faith,
may constantly devote themselves
to the service of the Gospel.
Keep us attentive to the needs of all
that, sharing their grief and pain,
their joy and hope,
we may faithfully bring them the good news of salvation
and go forward with them
along the way of your Kingdom.

Remember our brothers and sisters (N. and N.),
who have fallen asleep in the peace of your Christ,
and all the dead, whose faith you alone have known.
Admit them to rejoice in the light of your face,
and in the resurrection give them the fullness of life.

---

* Mention may be made here of the Coadjutor Bishop, or Auxiliary Bishops

Grant also to us,
when our earthly pilgrimage is done,
that we may come to an eternal dwelling place
and live with you for ever;
there, in communion with the Blessed Virgin Mary, Mother of God,
with the Apostles and Martyrs,
(with Saint N.: *the Saint of the day or Patron*)
and with all the Saints,
we shall praise and exalt you
through Jesus Christ, your Son.

Priest: Through him, and with him, and in him,   ▷ *Music p 18*
           O God, almighty Father,
           in the unity of the Holy Spirit,
           all glory and honour is yours,
           for ever and ever.
People: **Amen.**   ▷ *page 56*

IV   JESUS, WHO WENT ABOUT DOING GOOD

Priest: The Lord be with you.   ▷ *Music p 15*
People: **And with your spirit.**

Priest: Lift up your hearts.
People: **We lift them up to the Lord.**

Priest: Let us give thanks to the Lord our God.
People: **It is right and just.**

Priest: It is truly right and just, our duty and our salvation,
           always and everywhere to give you thanks,
           Father of mercies and faithful God.

           For you have given us Jesus Christ, your Son,
           as our Lord and Redeemer.

           He always showed compassion
           for children and for the poor,
           for the sick and for sinners,
           and he became a neighbour
           to the oppressed and the afflicted.

           By word and deed he announced to the world
           that you are our Father
           and that you care for all your sons and daughters.

           And so, with all the Angels and Saints,
           we exalt and bless your name
           and sing the hymn of your glory,
           as without end we acclaim:

All: **Holy, Holy, Holy Lord God of hosts.**   ▷ *Music p 16*
            Heaven and earth are full of your glory.
            Hosanna in the highest.
            Blessed is he who comes in the name of the Lord.
            Hosanna in the highest.

Priest: You are indeed Holy and to be glorified, O God,
            who love the human race
            and who always walk with us on the journey of life.
            Blessed indeed is your Son,
            present in our midst
            when we are gathered by his love
            and when, as once for the disciples, so now for us,
            he opens the Scriptures and breaks the bread.

Therefore, Father most merciful,
we ask that you send forth your Holy Spirit
to sanctify these gifts of bread and wine,
that they may become for us
the Body and ✠ Blood
of our Lord Jesus Christ.

On the day before he was to suffer,
on the night of the Last Supper,
he took bread and said the blessing,
broke the bread and gave it to his disciples, saying:

TAKE THIS, ALL OF YOU, AND EAT OF IT,
FOR THIS IS MY BODY,
WHICH WILL BE GIVEN UP FOR YOU.

In a similar way, when supper was ended,
he took the chalice, gave you thanks
and gave the chalice to his disciples, saying:

TAKE THIS, ALL OF YOU, AND DRINK FROM IT,
FOR THIS IS THE CHALICE OF MY BLOOD,
THE BLOOD OF THE NEW AND ETERNAL COVENANT,
WHICH WILL BE POURED OUT FOR YOU AND FOR MANY
FOR THE FORGIVENESS OF SINS.

DO THIS IN MEMORY OF ME.

Priest: The mystery of faith.   ▷ *Music p 17*

People: **We proclaim your Death, O Lord,**
and profess your Resurrection
until you come again.

or

People: **When we eat this Bread and drink this Cup,**
we proclaim your Death, O Lord,
until you come again.

or

People: **Save us, Saviour of the world,**
for by your Cross and Resurrection
you have set us free.

or   *for Ireland only:*

People: **My Lord and my God.**

Priest: Therefore, holy Father,
as we celebrate the memorial of Christ your Son, our Saviour,
whom you led through his Passion and Death on the Cross
to the glory of the Resurrection,
and whom you have seated at your right hand,
we proclaim the work of your love until he comes again
and we offer you the Bread of life
and the Chalice of blessing.

Look with favour on the oblation of your Church,
in which we show forth
the paschal Sacrifice of Christ that has been handed on to us,
and grant that, by the power of the Spirit of your love,
we may be counted now and until the day of eternity
among the members of your Son,
in whose Body and Blood we have communion.

Bring your Church, O Lord,
to perfect faith and charity,
together with N. our Pope and N. our Bishop,*
with all Bishops, Priests and Deacons,
and the entire people you have made your own.

Open our eyes
to the needs of our brothers and sisters;
inspire in us words and actions
to comfort those who labour and are burdened.
Make us serve them truly,
after the example of Christ and at his command.

---

* Mention may be made here of the Coadjutor Bishop, or Auxiliary Bishops

And may your Church stand as a living witness
to truth and freedom,
to peace and justice,
that all people may be raised up to a new hope.

Remember our brothers and sisters (N. and N.),
who have fallen asleep in the peace of your Christ,
and all the dead, whose faith you alone have known.
Admit them to rejoice in the light of your face,
and in the resurrection give them the fullness of life.

Grant also to us,
when our earthly pilgrimage is done,
that we may come to an eternal dwelling place
and live with you for ever;
there, in communion with the Blessed Virgin Mary, Mother of God,
with the Apostles and Martyrs,
(with Saint N.: *the Saint of the day or Patron*)
and with all the Saints,
we shall praise and exalt you
through Jesus Christ, your Son.

Priest: Through him, and with him, and in him,   ▷ *Music p 18*
          O God, almighty Father,
          in the unity of the Holy Spirit,
          all glory and honour is yours,
          for ever and ever.

People: **Amen.**

▷ *page 56*

> The eating and drinking together of the Lord's Body and Blood in a Paschal meal is the culmination of the Eucharist. The themes underlying these rites are the mutual love and reconciliation that are both the condition and the fruit of worthy communion and the unity of the many in the one.
>
> *Celebrating the Mass n 200*

ALL STAND

LORD'S PRAYER

Priest: At the Saviour's command
and formed by divine teaching,
we dare to say:

All: **Our Father, who art in heaven,**
hallowed be thy name;
thy kingdom come,
thy will be done
on earth as it is in heaven.
Give us this day our daily bread,
and forgive us our trespasses,
as we forgive those who trespass against us;
and lead us not into temptation,
but deliver us from evil.

▷ *Music p 215*

Priest: Deliver us, Lord, we pray, from every evil,
graciously grant peace in our days,
that, by the help of your mercy,
we may be always free from sin
and safe from all distress,
as we await the blessed hope
and the coming of our Saviour, Jesus Christ.

All: **For the kingdom,**
the power and the glory are yours
now and for ever.

RITE OF PEACE

Priest: Lord Jesus Christ,
who said to your Apostles,
Peace I leave you, my peace I give you,
look not on our sins,
but on the faith of your Church,
and graciously grant her peace and unity
in accordance with your will.
Who live and reign for ever and ever.

All: **Amen.**

Priest: The peace of the Lord be with you always.

All: **And with your spirit.**

▷ *Music p 215*

SIGN OF PEACE

The peace is always exchanged, though the invitation which introduces it is optional.

Deacon or Priest: Let us offer each other the sign of peace.

And all offer one another the customary sign of peace: a handclasp or handshake, which is an expression of peace, communion, and charity.

If commissioned ministers are to assist at Communion, it is desirable that they are in place on the sanctuary by the end of the exchange of peace. (Celebrating the Mass n 206)

BREAKING OF BREAD

The Priest takes the host, breaks it over the paten, and places a small piece into the chalice. Meanwhile the following is sung or said:

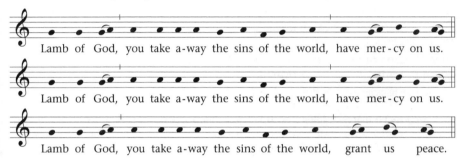

Lamb of God, you take a-way the sins of the world, have mer-cy on us.

Lamb of God, you take a-way the sins of the world, have mer-cy on us.

Lamb of God, you take a-way the sins of the world,   grant   us   peace.

All: **Lamb of God, you take away the sins of the world,
                have mercy on us.**

             **Lamb of God, you take away the sins of the world,
                have mercy on us.**

             **Lamb of God, you take away the sins of the world,
                grant us peace.**

*The invocation may be repeated several times if the Breaking of Bread is prolonged.
The final time always ends 'grant us peace'.*

ALL KNEEL

INVITATION TO COMMUNION

After his private prayers of preparation the Priest genuflects, takes the host and, holding it slightly raised above the paten or above the chalice says aloud:

Priest: Behold the Lamb of God,   ▷ *Music p 216*
               behold him who takes away the sins of the world.
               Blessed are those called to the supper of the Lamb.
All: **Lord, I am not worthy
               that you should enter under my roof,
               but only say the word
               and my soul shall be healed.**

HOLY COMMUNION

Communion Song

The communion song begins while the Priest is receiving the Body of Christ and normally continues until all communicants have received communion.

Distribution of Communion

By tradition the Deacon ministers the chalice. Beyond this, no distinctions are made in the assignment of consecrated elements to particular ministers for distribution. (Celebrating the Mass n 211)

The communicants come forward in reverent procession. Before receiving Holy Communion standing they make a preparatory act of reverence by bowing their heads in honour of Christ's presence in the Sacrament.

The Priest, Deacon or commissioned minister of Holy Communion raises a host slightly and shows it to each of the communicants, saying:

Priest, Deacon or minister: The Body of Christ.
Communicant: **Amen.**

And the communicant receives Holy Communion.

It is most desirable that the faithful share the Chalice. Drinking at the Eucharist is a sharing in the sign of the new covenant, a foretaste of the heavenly banquet and a sign of participation in the suffering Christ. (cf Celebrating the Mass n 209)

When Communion is ministered from the chalice, the minister offers it to each of the communicants, saying:

Priest, Deacon or minister: The Blood of Christ.
Communicant: **Amen.**

And the communicant receives Holy Communion.

Period of Silence or Song of Praise

After the distribution of Communion, if appropriate, a sacred silence may be observed for a while, or a psalm or other canticle of praise or a hymn may be sung.

PRAYER AFTER COMMUNION   **ALL STAND**

Priest: Let us pray.   ▷ **Proper**

All pray in silence for a while, unless silence has just been observed.
Then the Priest says the Prayer after Communion, at the end of which the people acclaim:

All: **Amen.**

CONCLUDING RITES

> *Go, make disciples of all the nations.*
> *I am with you always; yes, to the end of time.*
> (Matthew 28:19, 20)
>
> The purpose of the Concluding Rite is to send the people forth to put into effect in their daily lives the Paschal Mystery and the unity in Christ which they have celebrated. They are given a sense of abiding mission, which calls them to witness to Christ in the world and to bring the Gospel to the poor.
> *cf Celebrating the Mass n 217*

If they are necessary, any brief announcements to the people follow here.

BLESSING

Priest: The Lord be with you.   ▷ *Music p 217*
People: **And with your spirit.**

On certain occasions, the following blessing may be preceded by a solemn blessing or prayer over the people. Then the Priest blesses the people, singing or saying:
Priest: May almighty God bless you:
           the Father, and the Son, ✠ and the Holy Spirit.
People: **Amen.**

In a Pontifical Mass, the celebrant receives the mitre and says:
Bishop: The Lord be with you.   ▷ *Music p 217*
All: **And with your spirit.**

Bishop: Blessed be the name of the Lord.
All: **Now and for ever.**

Bishop: Our help is in the name of the Lord.
All   **Who made heaven and earth.**

On certain occasions the following blessing may be preceded by a more solemn blessing or prayer over the people. Then the celebrant receives the pastoral staff, if he uses it, and says:
Bishop: May almighty God bless you:
making the Sign of the Cross over the people three times, he adds:
           the Father, ✠ and the Son, ✠ and the Holy ✠ Spirit.
All: **Amen.**

If any liturgical action follows immediately, the rites of dismissal are omitted.

DISMISSAL

▷ *Music p 218*

Then the Deacon, or the Priest himself says the dismissal sentence.

Deacon or Priest: Go forth, the Mass is ended.
People: **Thanks be to God.**

or

Deacon or Priest: Go and announce the Gospel of the Lord.
People: **Thanks be to God.**

or

Deacon or Priest: Go in peace, glorifying the Lord by your life.
People: **Thanks be to God.**

or

Deacon or Priest: Go in peace.
People: **Thanks be to God.**

Then the Priest venerates the altar as at the beginning.
After making a profound bow with the ministers, he withdraws.

RITE FOR THE BLESSING AND SPRINKLING OF WATER

BLESSING OF WATER

After the greeting, the Priest, with a vessel containing the water to be blessed before him, calls upon the people to pray in these or similar words:

Priest: Dear brethren (brothers and sisters),
let us humbly beseech the Lord our God
to bless this water he has created,
which will be sprinkled on us
as a memorial of our Baptism.
May he help us by his grace
to remain faithful to the Spirit we have received.

And after a brief pause for silence, he continues:

Priest: Almighty ever-living God,
who willed that through water,
the fountain of life and the source of purification,
even souls should be cleansed
and receive the gift of eternal life;
be pleased, we pray, to ✠ bless this water,
by which we seek protection on this your day, O Lord.
Renew the living spring of your grace within us
and grant that by this water we may be defended
from all ills of spirit and body,
and so approach you with hearts made clean
and worthily receive your salvation.
Through Christ our Lord.

All: **Amen.**

or

Priest: Almighty Lord and God,
who are the source and origin of all life,
whether of body or soul,
we ask you to ✠ bless this water,
which we use in confidence
to implore forgiveness for our sins
and to obtain the protection of your grace
against all illness and every snare of the enemy.
Grant, O Lord, in your mercy,
that living waters may always spring up for our salvation,
and so may we approach you with a pure heart
and avoid all danger to body and soul.
Through Christ our Lord.

All: **Amen.**

BLESSING OF SALT

Where the circumstances of the place or the custom of the people suggest that the mixing of salt be preserved in the blessing of water, the Priest may bless salt, saying:

Priest: We humbly ask you, almighty God:
    be pleased in your faithful love to bless ✠ this salt
    you have created,
    for it was you who commanded the prophet Elisha
    to cast salt into water,
    that impure water might be purified.
    Grant, O Lord, we pray,
    that, wherever this mixture of salt and water is sprinkled,
    every attack of the enemy may be repulsed
    and your Holy Spirit may be present
    to keep us safe at all times.
    Through Christ our Lord.

All: **Amen.**

Then he pours the salt into the water.

SPRINKLING OF WATER

The Priest then sprinkles himself and the ministers, then the clergy and people, moving through the church, if appropriate.

Meanwhile, one of the following chants, or another appropriate song is sung.

ANTIPHON 1   *Psalm 50:9*

Sprinkle me with hyssop, O Lord, and I shall be cleansed;
wash me and I shall be whiter than snow.

ANTIPHON 2   *Ezekiel 36:25–26*

I will pour clean water upon you,
and you will be made clean of all your impurities,
and I shall give you a new spirit, says the Lord.

HYMN   *cf 1 Peter 1:3–5*

Blessed be the God and Father of our Lord Jesus Christ,
who in his great mercy has given us new birth into a living hope
through the Resurrection of Jesus Christ from the dead,
into an inheritance that will not perish,
preserved for us in heaven
for the salvation to be revealed in the last time!

PRAYER

When he returns to his chair and the singing is over, the Priest says:

Priest: May almighty God cleanse us of our sins,
    and through the celebration of this Eucharist
    make us worthy to share at the table of his Kingdom.

All: **Amen.**

The Mass continues with the Gloria.
If the Gloria is not indicated, the Mass continues with the Collect.

▷ page 9

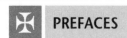

PREFACES

All the Prefaces within the scope of this volume are printed here, except those specific to a given Eucharistic Prayer (e.g. the Preface of Eucharistic Prayer II).

The Prefaces are printed in the order that the celebrations occur in the propers of this volume:

Proper of Time
Ordinary Time
• The Most Holy Trinity and Most Holy Body and Blood of Christ
• Sundays in Ordinary Time
• Our Lord Jesus Christ, King of the Universe

Proper of Saints

ORDINARY TIME — The Most Holy Trinity and Most Holy Body and Blood of Christ

The following Prefaces are said on specific occasions in Ordinary Time.

THE MYSTERY OF THE MOST HOLY TRINITY
This Preface is said on the Solemnity of The Most Holy Trinity.

It is truly right and just, our duty and our salvation,
always and everywhere to give you thanks,
Lord, holy Father, almighty and eternal God.

For with your Only Begotten Son and the Holy Spirit
you are one God, one Lord:
not in the unity of a single person,
but in a Trinity of one substance.

For what you have revealed to us of your glory
we believe equally of your Son
and of the Holy Spirit,
so that, in the confessing of the true and eternal Godhead,
you might be adored in what is proper to each Person,
their unity in substance,
and their equality in majesty.

For this is praised by Angels and Archangels,
Cherubim, too, and Seraphim,
who never cease to cry out each day,
as with one voice they acclaim:

Holy, Holy, Holy Lord God of hosts...

One of the Prefaces of the Most Holy Eucharist is said on the Solemnity of the Most Holy Body and Blood of Christ.

PREFACE I OF THE MOST HOLY EUCHARIST
THE SACRIFICE AND THE SACRAMENT OF CHRIST

It is truly right and just, our duty and our salvation,
always and everywhere to give you thanks,
Lord, holy Father, almighty and eternal God,
through Christ our Lord.

For he is the true and eternal Priest,
who instituted the pattern of an everlasting sacrifice
and was the first to offer himself as the saving Victim,
commanding us to make this offering as his memorial.
As we eat his flesh that was sacrificed for us,
we are made strong,
and, as we drink his Blood that was poured out for us,
we are washed clean.

And so, with Angels and Archangels,
with Thrones and Dominions,
and with all the hosts and Powers of heaven,
we sing the hymn of your glory,
as without end we acclaim:

Holy, Holy, Holy Lord God of hosts...

PREFACE II OF THE MOST HOLY EUCHARIST
THE FRUITS OF THE MOST HOLY EUCHARIST

It is truly right and just, our duty and our salvation,
always and everywhere to give you thanks,
Lord, holy Father, almighty and eternal God,
through Christ our Lord.

For at the Last Supper with his Apostles,
establishing for the ages to come the saving memorial of the Cross,
he offered himself to you as the unblemished Lamb,
the acceptable gift of perfect praise.

Nourishing your faithful by this sacred mystery,
you make them holy, so that the human race,
bounded by one world,
may be enlightened by one faith
and united by one bond of charity.

And so, we approach the table of this wondrous Sacrament,
so that, bathed in the sweetness of your grace,
we may pass over to the heavenly realities here foreshadowed.

Therefore, all creatures of heaven and earth
sing a new song in adoration,
and we, with all the host of Angels,
cry out, and without end we acclaim:

Holy, Holy, Holy Lord God of hosts...

APPENDIX

ORDINARY TIME — Sundays in Ordinary Time

The following Prefaces are said on Sundays in Ordinary Time which do not have a proper Preface.

PREFACE I
OF THE SUNDAYS IN ORDINARY TIME

THE PASCHAL MYSTERY
AND THE PEOPLE OF GOD

It is truly right and just,
    our duty and our salvation,
always and everywhere to give you thanks,
Lord, holy Father, almighty
    and eternal God,
through Christ our Lord.

For through his Paschal Mystery,
he accomplished the marvellous deed,
by which he has freed us
    from the yoke of sin and death,
summoning us to the glory
    of being now called
a chosen race, a royal priesthood,
a holy nation, a people
    for your own possession,
to proclaim everywhere your mighty works,
for you have called us out of darkness
into your own wonderful light.

And so, with Angels and Archangels,
with Thrones and Dominions,
and with all the hosts
    and Powers of heaven,
we sing the hymn of your glory,
as without end we acclaim:

Holy, Holy, Holy Lord God of hosts…

PREFACE III
OF THE SUNDAYS IN ORDINARY TIME

THE SALVATION OF MAN BY A MAN

It is truly right and just,
    our duty and our salvation,
always and everywhere to give you thanks,
Lord, holy Father,
    almighty and eternal God.

For we know it belongs
    to your boundless glory,
that you came to the aid of mortal beings
    with your divinity

PREFACE II
OF THE SUNDAYS IN ORDINARY TIME

THE MYSTERY OF SALVATION

It is truly right and just,
    our duty and our salvation,
always and everywhere to give you thanks,
Lord, holy Father,
    almighty and eternal God,
through Christ our Lord.

For out of compassion for the waywardness
    that is ours,
he humbled himself
    and was born of the Virgin;
by the passion of the Cross
    he freed us from unending death,
and by rising from the dead
    he gave us life eternal.

And so, with Angels and Archangels,
with Thrones and Dominions,
and with all the hosts
    and Powers of heaven,
we sing the hymn of your glory,
as without end we acclaim:

Holy, Holy, Holy Lord God of hosts…

and even fashioned for us
    a remedy out of mortality itself,
that the cause of our downfall
might become the means of our salvation,
through Christ our Lord.

Through him the host of Angels
    adores your majesty
and rejoices in your presence for ever.
May our voices, we pray, join with theirs
in one chorus of exultant praise,
    as we acclaim:

Holy, Holy, Holy Lord God of hosts…

PREFACE IV
OF THE SUNDAYS IN ORDINARY TIME
THE HISTORY OF SALVATION

It is truly right and just,
    our duty and our salvation,
always and everywhere to give you thanks,
Lord, holy Father,
    almighty and eternal God,
through Christ our Lord.

For by his birth he brought renewal
to humanity's fallen state,
and by his suffering cancelled out our sins;
by his rising from the dead
he has opened the way to eternal life,
and by ascending to you, O Father,
he has unlocked the gates of heaven.

And so, with the company
    of Angels and Saints,
we sing the hymn of your praise,
as without end we acclaim:

Holy, Holy, Holy Lord God of hosts...

PREFACE V
OF THE SUNDAYS IN ORDINARY TIME
CREATION

It is truly right and just,
    our duty and our salvation,
always and everywhere to give you thanks,
Lord, holy Father,
    almighty and eternal God.

For you laid the foundations of the world
and have arranged the changing
    of times and seasons;
you formed man in your own image
and set humanity over the whole world
    in all its wonder,
to rule in your name over all
    you have made
and for ever praise you
    in your mighty works,
through Christ our Lord.

And so, with all the Angels, we praise you,
as in joyful celebration we acclaim:

Holy, Holy, Holy Lord God of hosts...

PREFACE VI
OF THE SUNDAYS IN ORDINARY TIME
THE PLEDGE OF THE ETERNAL PASSOVER

It is truly right and just,
    our duty and our salvation,
always and everywhere to give you thanks,
Lord, holy Father,
    almighty and eternal God.

For in you we live and move
    and have our being,
and while in this body
we not only experience the daily effects
    of your care,
but even now possess the pledge
    of life eternal.

For, having received the first fruits
    of the Spirit,
through whom you raised up Jesus
    from the dead,
we hope for an everlasting share
    in the Paschal Mystery.

And so, with all the Angels, we praise you,
as in joyful celebration we acclaim:

Holy, Holy, Holy Lord God of hosts...

PREFACE VII
OF THE SUNDAYS IN ORDINARY TIME
SALVATION THROUGH
THE OBEDIENCE OF CHRIST

It is truly right and just,
    our duty and our salvation,
always and everywhere to give you thanks,
Lord, holy Father,
    almighty and eternal God.

For you so loved the world
that in your mercy you sent us the Redeemer,
to live like us in all things but sin,
so that you might love in us
    what you loved in your Son,
by whose obedience we have been restored
    to those gifts of yours
that, by sinning, we had lost
    in disobedience.

And so, Lord, with all the Angels and Saints,
we, too, give you thanks,
    as in exultation we acclaim:

Holy, Holy, Holy Lord God of hosts...

APPENDIX

PREFACE VIII OF THE SUNDAYS IN ORDINARY TIME

THE CHURCH UNITED BY THE UNITY OF THE TRINITY

It is truly right and just,
   our duty and our salvation,
always and everywhere to give you thanks,
Lord, holy Father,
   almighty and eternal God.

For, when your children were scattered afar
   by sin,
through the Blood of your Son
   and the power of the Spirit,
you gathered them again to yourself,
that a people, formed as one
   by the unity of the Trinity,

made the body of Christ
   and the temple of the Holy Spirit,
might, to the praise
   of your manifold wisdom,
be manifest as the Church.

And so, in company with
   the choirs of Angels,
we praise you, and with joy we proclaim:

Holy, Holy, Holy Lord God of hosts...

ORDINARY TIME — Our Lord Jesus Christ, King of the Universe

CHRIST, KING OF THE UNIVERSE

This Preface is said on the Solemnity of Our Lord Jesus Christ, King of the Universe.

It is truly right and just, our duty and our salvation,
always and everywhere to give you thanks,
Lord, holy Father, almighty and eternal God.

For you anointed your Only Begotten Son,
our Lord Jesus Christ, with the oil of gladness
as eternal Priest and King of all creation,
so that, by offering himself on the altar of the Cross
as a spotless sacrifice to bring us peace,
he might accomplish the mysteries of human redemption
and, making all created things subject to his rule,
he might present to the immensity of your majesty
an eternal and universal kingdom,
a kingdom of truth and life,
a kingdom of holiness and grace,
a kingdom of justice, love and peace.

And so, with Angels and Archangels,
with Thrones and Dominions,
and with all the hosts and Powers of heaven,
we sing the hymn of your glory,
as without end we acclaim:

Holy, Holy, Holy Lord God of hosts...

PROPER OF SAINTS

These Prefaces are said in Masses from the Proper of Saints.

THE MISSION OF THE PRECURSOR

The following Preface is said on the Solemnity of the Nativity of John the Baptist (24 June).

It is truly right and just,
      our duty and our salvation,
always and everywhere to give you thanks,
Lord, holy Father,
      almighty and eternal God,
through Christ our Lord.

In his Precursor, Saint John the Baptist,
we praise your great glory,
for you consecrated him
      for a singular honour
among those born of women.

His birth brought great rejoicing;
even in the womb he leapt for joy
at the coming of human salvation.
He alone of all the prophets
pointed out the Lamb of redemption.

And to make holy the flowing waters,
he baptized the very author of Baptism
and was privileged to bear him
      supreme witness
by the shedding of his blood.

And so, with the Powers of heaven,
we worship you constantly on earth,
and before your majesty
without end we acclaim:

Holy, Holy, Holy Lord God of hosts...

THE TWOFOLD MISSION OF PETER AND PAUL IN THE CHURCH

The following Preface is said on the Solemnity of Saints Peter and Paul (29 June).

It is truly right and just,
      our duty and our salvation,
always and everywhere to give you thanks,
Lord, holy Father,
      almighty and eternal God.

For by your providence
the blessed Apostles Peter and Paul
      bring us joy:
Peter, foremost in confessing the faith,
Paul, its outstanding preacher,
Peter, who established the early Church
      from the remnant of Israel,
Paul, master and teacher of the Gentiles
      that you call.

And so, each in a different way
gathered together the one family of Christ;
and revered together throughout the world,
they share one Martyr's crown.

And therefore, with all the Angels
      and Saints,
we praise you, as without end we acclaim:

Holy, Holy, Holy Lord God of hosts...

APPENDIX

THE MYSTERY OF THE TRANSFIGURATION

The following Preface is said on the Feast of the Transfiguration of the Lord (6 August).

It is truly right and just,
  our duty and our salvation,
always and everywhere to give you thanks,
Lord, holy Father,
  almighty and eternal God,
through Christ our Lord.

For he revealed his glory
  in the presence of chosen witnesses
and filled with the greatest splendour
  that bodily form
which he shares with all humanity,
that the scandal of the Cross
might be removed from the hearts
  of his disciples
and that he might show
how in the Body of the whole Church
  is to be fulfilled
what so wonderfully shone forth
  first in its Head.

And so, with the Powers of heaven,
we worship you constantly on earth,
and before your majesty
without end we acclaim:

Holy, Holy, Holy Lord God of hosts...

THE GLORY OF MARY ASSUMED INTO HEAVEN

The following Preface is said on the Solemnity of The Assumption of the Blessed Virgin Mary (15 August).

It is truly right and just,
  our duty and our salvation,
always and everywhere to give you thanks,
Lord, holy Father,
  almighty and eternal God,
through Christ our Lord.

For today the Virgin Mother of God
was assumed into heaven
as the beginning and image
of your Church's coming to perfection
and a sign of sure hope and comfort
  to your pilgrim people;
rightly you would not allow her
to see the corruption of the tomb
since from her own body
  she marvellously brought forth
your incarnate Son, the Author of all life.

And so, in company
  with the choirs of Angels,
we praise you, and with joy we proclaim:

Holy, Holy, Holy Lord God of hosts...

Either of the following two Prefaces may be said on the Feast of the Exaltation of the Holy Cross (14 September).

THE VICTORY OF THE GLORIOUS CROSS

It is truly right and just,
  our duty and our salvation,
always and everywhere to give you thanks,
Lord, holy Father,
  almighty and eternal God.

For you placed the salvation of
  the human race
on the wood of the Cross,
so that, where death arose,
life might again spring forth
and the evil one, who conquered on a tree,
might likewise on a tree be conquered,
through Christ our Lord.

Through him the Angels
  praise your majesty,
Dominions adore and Powers
  tremble before you.
Heaven and the Virtues of heaven
  and the blessed Seraphim
worship together with exultation.

May our voices, we pray, join with theirs
in humble praise, as we acclaim:

Holy, Holy, Holy Lord God of hosts...

PREFACE I
OF THE PASSION OF THE LORD
THE POWER OF THE CROSS

It is truly right and just,
      our duty and our salvation,
always and everywhere to give you thanks,
Lord, holy Father,
      almighty and eternal God.

For through the saving Passion of your Son
the whole world has received a heart
to confess the infinite power
      of your majesty,

since by the wondrous power of the Cross
your judgement on the world
      is now revealed
and the authority of Christ crucified.

And so, Lord, with all the Angels and Saints,
we, too, give you thanks,
      as in exultation we acclaim:

Holy, Holy, Holy Lord God of hosts...

THE GLORY OF JERUSALEM, OUR MOTHER

This Preface is said on the Solemnity of All Saints (1 November).

It is truly right and just,
      our duty and our salvation,
always and everywhere to give you thanks,
Lord, holy Father,
      almighty and eternal God.

For today by your gift we celebrate
      the festival of your city,
the heavenly Jerusalem, our mother,
where the great array of
      our brothers and sisters
already gives you eternal praise.

Towards her, we eagerly hasten,
      as pilgrims advancing by faith,
rejoicing in the glory bestowed upon
      those exalted members of the Church
through whom you give us, in our frailty,
      both strength and good example.

And so, we glorify you with the multitude
      of Saints and Angels,
as with one voice of praise we acclaim:

Holy, Holy, Holy Lord God of hosts...

The following Prefaces are said in Masses for the Dead including the Commemoration of All the Faithful Departed (All Souls' Day) (2 November).

PREFACE I FOR THE DEAD
THE HOPE OF RESURRECTION IN CHRIST

It is truly right and just,
      our duty and our salvation,
always and everywhere to give you thanks,
Lord, holy Father,
      almighty and eternal God,
through Christ our Lord.

In him the hope of blessed resurrection
      has dawned,
that those saddened by the certainty
      of dying
might be consoled by the promise
      of immortality to come.

Indeed for your faithful, Lord,
life is changed not ended,
and, when this earthly dwelling
      turns to dust,
an eternal dwelling is made ready
      for them in heaven.

And so, with Angels and Archangels,
with Thrones and Dominions,
and with all the hosts and Powers of heaven,
we sing the hymn of your glory,
as without end we acclaim:

Holy, Holy, Holy Lord God of hosts...

PREFACE II FOR THE DEAD
CHRIST DIED SO THAT WE MIGHT LIVE

It is truly right and just,
    our duty and our salvation,
always and everywhere to give you thanks,
Lord, holy Father,
    almighty and eternal God,
through Christ our Lord.

For as one alone he accepted death,
so that we might all escape from dying;
as one man he chose to die,
so that in your sight
    we all might live for ever.

And so, in company
    with the choirs of Angels,
we praise you, and with joy we proclaim:

Holy, Holy, Holy Lord God of hosts...

PREFACE III FOR THE DEAD
CHRIST, THE SALVATION AND THE LIFE
It is truly right and just,
    our duty and our salvation,
always and everywhere to give you thanks,
Lord, holy Father,
    almighty and eternal God,
through Christ our Lord.

For he is the salvation of the world,
the life of the human race,
the resurrection of the dead.

Through him the host of Angels
    adores your majesty
and rejoices in your presence for ever.
May our voices, we pray, join with theirs
in one chorus of exultant praise,
    as we acclaim:

Holy, Holy, Holy Lord God of hosts...

PREFACE IV FOR THE DEAD
FROM EARTHLY LIFE TO HEAVENLY GLORY

It is truly right and just,
    our duty and our salvation,
always and everywhere to give you thanks,
Lord, holy Father,
    almighty and eternal God.

For it is at your summons
    that we come to birth,
by your will that we are governed,
and at your command that we return,
on account of sin,
to the earth from which we came.

And when you give the sign,
we who have been redeemed
    by the Death of your Son,
shall be raised up to the glory
    of his Resurrection.

And so, with the company
    of Angels and Saints,
we sing the hymn of your praise,
as without end we acclaim:

Holy, Holy, Holy Lord God of hosts...

PREFACE V FOR THE DEAD
OUR RESURRECTION THROUGH THE VICTORY
OF CHRIST

It is truly right and just,
    our duty and our salvation,
always and everywhere to give you thanks,
Lord, holy Father,
    almighty and eternal God.

For even though by our own fault
    we perish,
yet by your compassion and your grace,
when seized by death according to our sins,
we are redeemed
    through Christ's great victory,
and with him called back into life.

And so, with the Powers of heaven,
we worship you constantly on earth,
and before your majesty
without end we acclaim:

Holy, Holy, Holy Lord God of hosts...

THE MYSTERY OF THE CHURCH, THE BRIDE OF CHRIST AND THE TEMPLE OF THE SPIRIT

This Preface is said on the Feast of the Dedication of the Lateran Basilica (9 November).

It is truly right and just,
  our duty and our salvation,
always and everywhere to give you thanks,
Lord, holy Father,
  almighty and eternal God.

For in your benevolence you are pleased
to dwell in this house of prayer
in order to perfect us as the temple
  of the Holy Spirit,

supported by the perpetual help
  of your grace
and resplendent with the glory
  of a life acceptable to you.

Year by year you sanctify the Church,
  the Bride of Christ,
foreshadowed in visible buildings,
so that, rejoicing as the mother
  of countless children,
she may be given her place
  in your heavenly glory.

And so, with all the Angels and Saints,
we praise you, as without end
  we acclaim:

Holy, Holy, Holy Lord God of hosts...

LATIN TEXTS OF THE ORDER OF MASS

CONFITEOR

Confiteor Deo omnipotenti et vobis, fratres,
quia peccavi nimis
cogitatione, verbo, opere et omissione:
mea culpa, mea culpa, mea maxima culpa.
Ideo precor beatam Mariam semper Virginem,
omnes Angelos et Sanctos,
et vos, fratres, orare pro me
ad Dominum Deum nostrum. Amen

KYRIE

Kyrie, eleison
Kyrie, eleison.

Christe, eleison.
Christe, eleison.

Kyrie, eleison.
Kyrie, eleison.

GLORIA

Gloria in excelsis Deo
et in terra pax hominibus bonae voluntatis.
Laudamus te,
benedicimus te,
adoramus te,
glorificamus te,
gratias agimus tibi propter magnam
  gloriam tuam,
Domine Deus, Rex caelestis,
Deus Pater omnipotens.

Domine Fili unigenite, Jesu Christe,
Domine Deus, Agnus Dei, Filius Patris,
qui tollis peccata mundi, miserere nobis;
qui tollis peccata mundi,
  suscipe deprecationem nostram.
Qui sedes ad dexteram Patris,
  miserere nobis.
Quoniam tu solus Sanctus,
  tu solus Dominus,
tu solus Altissimus,
Jesu Christe, cum Sancto Spiritu:
  in gloria Dei Patris. Amen.

CREDO

Credo in unum Deum,
Patrem Omnipotentem,
  factorem caeli et terrae,
visibilium omnium et invisibilium.
Et in unum Dominum Jesum Christum,
Filium Dei unigenitum,
  et ex Patre natum ante omnia saecula.
Deum de Deo, lumen de lumine,
  Deum verum de Deo vero,
genitum, non factum,
  consubstantialem Patri:
per quem omnia facta sunt.
Qui propter nos homines
  et propter nostram salutem
descendit de caelis.

Et incarnatus est de Spiritu Sancto
ex Maria Virgine; et homo factus est.

Crucifixus etiam pro nobis sub Pontio Pilato;
passus et sepultus est,
et resurrexit tertia die, secundum Scripturas,
et ascendit in caelum,
    sedet ad dexteram Patris.
Et iterum venturus est cum gloria,
    iudicare vivos et mortuos,
cuius regni non erit finis.
Et in Spiritum Sanctum,
    Dominum et vivificantem:
qui ex Patre Filioque procedit.
Qui cum Patre et Filio simul adoratur
    et conglorificatur:
qui locutus est per prophetas.
Et unam, sanctam, catholicam
    et apostolicam Ecclesiam.
Confiteor unum baptisma
    in remissionem peccatorum.
Et exspecto resurrectionem mortuorum,
et vitam venturi saeculi. Amen.

ORATE FRATRES
Orate fratres:
ut meum ac vestrum sacrificium
acceptabile fiat apud Deum
    Patrem omnipotentem.

Suscipiat Dominus sacrificium
    de manibus tuis
ad laudem et gloriam nominis sui,
ad utilitatem quoque nostram
totiusque Ecclesiae sanctae.

SURSUM CORDA
Dominus vobiscum.
Et cum spiritu tuo.

Sursum corda.
Habemus ad Dominum.

Gratias agamus Domine Deo nostro.
Dignum et iustum est.

SANCTUS
Sanctus, Sanctus, Sanctus Dominus
    Deus Sabaoth.
Pleni sunt caeli et terra gloria tua.
Hosanna in excelsis.
Benedictus qui venit in nomine Domini.
Hosanna in excelsis.

MYSTERIUM FIDEI
Mysterium Fidei.
1 **Mortem tuam annuntiamus, Domine,**
   et tuam resurrectionem confitemur,
     donec venias.

2 **Quotiescumque manducamus panem**
    hunc
   et calicem bibimus
   mortem tuam annuntiamus, Domine,
    donec venias.

3 **Salvator mundi, salva nos,**
   aui per crucem et resurrectionem tuam
    liberasti nos.

PATER NOSTER
Praeceptis salutaribus moniti,
et divina insitutione formati,
audemus dicere:

Pater noster, qui es in caelis:
sanctificetur nomen tuum;
adveniat regnum tuum;
fiat voluntas tua, sicut in caelo,
    et in terra.
Panem nostrum cotidianum
    da nobis hodie;
et dimitte nobis debita nostra,
sicut et nos dimittimus debitoribus
    nostris
et ne nos inducas in tentationem;
sed libera nos a malo.

Libera nos, quaesumus, Domine,
    ab omnibus malis,...
...et adventum Salvatoris nostri Iesu Christi.

Quia tuum est regnum,
et potestas, et gloria
in saecula.

AGNUS DEI
Agnus Dei, qui tollis peccata mundi:
    miserere nobis.
Agnus Dei, qui tollis peccata mundi:
    miserere nobis.
Agnus Dei, qui tollis peccata mundi:
    dona nobis pacem.

CONTENTS OF THE PROPER OF TIME

COMMON RESPONSORIAL PSALMS

The Responsorial Psalm should correspond to each reading and should, as a rule, be taken from the Lectionary In order, however, that the people may be able to sing the Psalm response more readily, texts of some responses and psalms have been chosen for the various seasons of the year or for the various categories of Saints. These may be used in place of the text corresponding to the reading whenever the Psalm is sung.

General Instruction of the Roman Missal n 61

The Common Responsorial Psalms for Ordinary Time begin on the following page.

 ORDINARY TIME

ABOUT THE SEASON

Besides the times of year that have their own distinctive character, there remain in the yearly cycle thirty-three or thirty-four weeks in which no particular aspect of the mystery of Christ is celebrated, but rather the mystery of Christ itself is honoured in its fullness, especially on Sundays. This period is known as Ordinary Time.

Universal Norms on the Liturgical Year and the Calendar n 43

ABOUT THE READINGS

On the Second Sunday of Ordinary Time the gospel continues to centre on the manifestation of the Lord, which Epiphany celebrates through the traditional passage about the wedding feast at Cana and two other passages from John.

Beginning with the Third Sunday, there is a semi-continuous reading of the Synoptic Gospels. This reading is arranged in such a way that as the Lord's life and preaching unfold the teaching proper to each of these Gospels is presented.

This distribution also provides a certain co-ordination between the meaning of each Gospel and the progress of the liturgical year. Thus after Epiphany the readings are on the beginning of the Lord's preaching and they fit in well with Christ's baptism and the first events in which he manifests himself. The liturgical year leads quite naturally to a termination in the eschatological theme proper to the last Sundays, since the chapters of the Synoptics that precede the account of the passion treat this eschatological theme rather extensively.

Introduction to the Lectionary n 105

COMMON RESPONSORIAL PSALMS FOR ORDINARY TIME

COMMON RESPONSES

WITH A PSALM OF PRAISE

> O give thanks to the Lord for he is good.

or

> We thank you, Lord, for the wonders of all your creation.

or

> O sing a new song to the Lord

WITH A PSALM OF PETITION

> The Lord is close to all who call him.

or

> Pay heed to us, Lord, and save us.

or

> The Lord is compassion and love.

COMMON PSALM 1   *Psalm 18:8–11 response John 6:68; alternative response John 6:63*

> **Lord, you have the message of eternal life.**
>
> *or*
>
> **Your words, Lord, are spirit and they are life.**

1 The law of the Lord is perfect,
it revives the soul.
The rule of the Lord is to be trusted,
it gives wisdom to the simple.

2 The precepts of the Lord are right,
they gladden the heart.
The command of the Lord is clear,
it gives light to the eyes.

3 The fear of the Lord is holy,
abiding for ever.
The decrees of the Lord are truth
and all of them just.

4 They are more to be desired than gold,
than the purest of gold
and sweeter are they than honey,
than honey from the comb.

COMMON PSALM 2   *Psalm 26:1, 4, 13–14 response v 1*

> **The Lord is my light and my help.**

1 The Lord is my light and my help;
whom shall I fear?
The Lord is the stronghold of my life;
before whom shall I shrink?

2 There is one thing I ask of the Lord,
for this I long,
to live in the house of the Lord,
all the days of my life,
to savour the sweetness of the Lord,
to behold his temple.

3 I am sure I shall see the Lord's goodness
in the land of the living.
Hope in him, hold firm and take heart.
Hope in the Lord!

COMMON PSALM 3 *Psalm 33:2–9 response v 2; alternative response v 9*

I will bless the Lord at all times.   *or*   **Taste and see that the Lord is good.**

1 I will bless the Lord at all times,
   his praise always on my lips;
   in the Lord my soul shall make its boast.
   The humble shall hear and be glad.

2 Glorify the Lord with me.
   Together let us praise his name
   I sought the Lord and he answered me;
   from all my terrors he set me free.

3 Look towards him and be radiant;
   let your faces not be abashed.
   This poor man called; the Lord heard him
   and rescued him from all his distress.

4 The angel of the Lord is encamped
   around those who revere him, to rescue them.
   Taste and see that the Lord is good.
   He is happy who seeks refuge in him.

COMMON PSALM 4 *Psalm 62:2–6, 8–9 response v 2*

For you my soul is thirsting, O Lord, my God.

1 O God, you are my God, for you I long;
   for you my soul is thirsting.
   My body pines for you
   like a dry, weary land without water.

2 So I gaze on you in the sanctuary
   to see your strength and your glory.
   For your love is better than life,
   my lips will speak your praise.

3 So I will bless you all my life,
   in your name I will lift up my hands.
   My soul shall be filled as with a banquet,
   my mouth shall praise you with joy.

4 For you have been my help;
   in the shadow of your wings I rejoice.
   My soul clings to you;
   your right hand holds me fast.

COMMON PSALM 5 *Psalm 94:1–2, 6–9 response vv 7–8*

**O that today you would listen to his voice!
Harden not your hearts.**

1 Come, ring out our joy to the Lord;
   hail the rock who saves us.
   Let us come before him, giving thanks,
   with songs let us hail the Lord.

2 Come in; let us bow and bend low,
   let us kneel before the God who made us
   for he is our God and we
   the people who belong to his pasture,
   the flock that is led by his hand.

3 O that today you would listen to his voice!
   'Harden not your hearts as at Meribah,
   as on that day at Massah in the desert
   when your fathers put me to the test;
   when they tried me, though they saw my work.'

COMMON PSALM 6   *Psalm 99:1–3, 5 response v 3*

We are his people, the sheep of his flock.

1 Cry out with joy to the Lord, all the earth.
   Serve the Lord with gladness.
   Come before him, singing for joy.

2 Know that he, the Lord, is God.
   He made us, we belong to him,
   we are his people, the sheep of his flock.

3 Indeed, how good is the Lord,
   eternal his merciful love.
   He is faithful from age to age.

COMMON PSALM 7   *Psalm 102:1–4, 8, 10, 12–13 response v 8*

The Lord is compassion and love.

1 My soul, give thanks to the Lord,
   all my being, bless his holy name.
   My soul, give thanks to the Lord
   and never forget all his blessings.

2 It is he who forgives all your guilt,
   who heals every one of your ills,
   who redeems your life from the grave,
   who crowns you with love and compassion.

3 The Lord is compassion and love,
   slow to anger and rich in mercy.
   He does not treat us according to our sins
   nor repay us according to our faults.

4 As far as the east is from the west
   so far does he remove our sins.
   As a father has compassion on his sons,
   the Lord has pity on those who fear him.

ORDINARY

COMMON PSALM 8   *Psalm 144:1–2, 8–11, 13–14 response cf v 1*

I will bless your name for ever, O God my King.

1   I will give you glory, O God my King,
    I will bless your name for ever.
    I will bless you day after day
    and praise your name for ever.

2   The Lord is kind and full of compassion,
    slow to anger, abounding in love.
    How good is the Lord to all,
    compassionate to all his creatures.

3   All your creatures shall thank you, O Lord,
    and your friends shall repeat their blessing.
    They shall speak of the glory of your reign
    and declare your might, O God.

4   The Lord is faithful in all his words
    and loving in all his deeds.
    The Lord supports all who fall
    and raises all who are bowed down.

COMMON PSALM 9   **For the Last Weeks of the Year**   *Psalm 121:1–9 response v 1*

Let us go to God's house, rejoicing.

1   I rejoiced when I heard them say:
    'Let us go to God's house.'
    And now our feet are standing
    within your gates, O Jerusalem.

2   Jerusalem is built as a city
    strongly compact.
    It is there that the tribes go up,
    the tribes of the Lord.

3   For Israel's law it is,
    there to praise the Lord's name.
    There were set the thrones of judgment
    of the house of David.

4   For the peace of Jerusalem pray:
    'Peace be to your homes!
    May peace reign in your walls,
    in your palaces, peace!'

5   For love of my brethren and friends
    I say: 'Peace upon you!'
    For love of the house of the Lord
    I will ask for your good.

MOST HOLY TRINITY

FIRST SUNDAY AFTER PENTECOST

ENTRANCE ANTIPHON
Blest be God the Father,
and the Only Begotten Son of God,
and also the Holy Spirit,
for he has shown us his merciful love.

▷ *page 7*

COLLECT
God our Father, who by sending into the world
the Word of truth and the Spirit of sanctification
made known to the human race your wondrous mystery,
grant us, we pray, that in professing the true faith,
we may acknowledge the Trinity of eternal glory
and adore your Unity, powerful in majesty.
Through our Lord Jesus Christ, your Son,
who lives and reigns with you in the unity of the Holy Spirit,
one God, for ever and ever. **Amen.**

FIRST READING *Exodus 34:4–6, 8–9*
Lord, Lord, a God of tenderness and compassion.

With the two tablets of stone in his hands, Moses went up the mountain of Sinai in the early morning as the Lord had commanded him. And the Lord descended in the form of a cloud, and Moses stood with him there.

He called on the name of the Lord. The Lord passed before him and proclaimed, 'Lord, Lord, a God of tenderness and compassion, slow to anger, rich in kindness and faithfulness.' And Moses bowed down to the ground at once and worshipped. 'If I have indeed won your favour, Lord,' he said 'let my Lord come with us, I beg. True, they are a headstrong people, but forgive us our faults and our sins, and adopt us as your heritage.'

The word of the Lord.
Thanks be to God.

RESPONSORIAL PSALM *Daniel 3:52–56, response v 52*

The response is sung after every line.

1 You are blest, Lord God of our fathers.
   To you glory and praise for evermore.
   Blest your glorious holy name.
   To you glory and praise for evermore.

2 You are blest in the temple of your glory.
   To you glory and praise for evermore.
   You are blest on the throne of your kingdom.
   To you glory and praise for evermore.

continued…

ORDINARY

3   You are blest who gaze into the depths.
    To you glory and praise for evermore.
    You are blest in the firmament of heaven.
    To you glory and praise for evermore.

SECOND READING   2 Corinthians 13:11–13

The grace of Jesus Christ, the love of God, and the fellowship of the Holy Spirit.

Brothers, we wish you happiness; try to grow perfect; help one another. Be united; live in peace, and the God of love and peace will be with you.

Greet one another with the holy kiss. All the saints send you greetings.

The grace of the Lord Jesus Christ, the love of God and the fellowship of the Holy Spirit be with you all.

The word of the Lord.
Thanks be to God.

GOSPEL ACCLAMATION   cf Apocalypse 1:8

Alleluia, alleluia!
Glory be to the Father, and to the Son, and to the Holy Spirit,
the God who is, who was, and who is to come.
Alleluia!

GOSPEL   John 3:16–18

The Lord be with you.
And with your spirit.

A reading from the holy Gospel according to John.
Glory to you, O Lord.

God sent his Son so that through him the world might be saved.

Jesus said to Nicodemus,

'God loved the world so much that he gave his only Son, so that everyone who believes in him may not be lost but may have eternal life. For God sent his Son into the world not to condemn the world, but so that through him the world might be saved. No one who believes in him will be condemned; but whoever refuses to believe is condemned already, because he has refused to believe in the name of God's only Son.'

The Gospel of the Lord.
Praise to you, Lord Jesus Christ.

▷ page 11

PRAYER OVER THE OFFERINGS

Sanctify by the invocation of your name,
we pray, O Lord our God,
this oblation of our service,
and by it make of us an eternal offering to you.
Through Christ our Lord. **Amen.**

▷ page 15

Preface of The Mystery of the Most Holy Trinity, page 64.

COMMUNION ANTIPHON   *Galatians 4:6*

Since you are children of God,
God has sent into your hearts the Spirit of his Son,
the Spirit who cries out: Abba, Father.

▷ *page 58*

PRAYER AFTER COMMUNION

May receiving this Sacrament, O Lord our God,
bring us health of body and soul,
as we confess your eternal holy Trinity and undivided Unity.
Through Christ our Lord.   **Amen.**

▷ *page 59*

ORDINARY

MOST HOLY BODY AND BLOOD OF CHRIST

(CORPUS CHRISTI)
THURSDAY AFTER THE MOST HOLY TRINITY

*When the Solemnity of the Most Holy Body and Blood of Christ is not a Holyday of Obligation,
it is assigned to the Sunday after the Most Holy Trinity as its proper day.*

ENTRANCE ANTIPHON   *cf Psalm 80:17*

He fed them with the finest wheat
and satisfied them with honey from the rock.

▷ *page 7*

COLLECT

O God, who in this wonderful Sacrament
have left us a memorial of your Passion,
grant us, we pray,
so to revere the sacred mysteries of your Body and Blood
that we may always experience in ourselves
the fruits of your redemption.
Who live and reign with God the Father
in the unity of the Holy Spirit,
one God, for ever and ever.   **Amen.**

FIRST READING   *Deuteronomy 8:2–3,14–16*

*He fed you with manna which neither you nor your
fathers had known.*

Moses said to the people: 'Remember
how the Lord your God led you for
forty years in the wilderness, to humble
you, to test you and know your inmost
heart – whether you would keep his
commandments or not. He humbled
you, he made you feel hunger, he fed
you with manna which neither you
nor your fathers had known, to make
you understand that man does not live
on bread alone but that man lives on
everything that comes from the mouth
of the Lord.

'Do not then forget the Lord your
God who brought you out of the land
of Egypt, out of the house of slavery:
who guided you through this vast and

dreadful wilderness, a land of fiery serpents, scorpions, thirst; who in this waterless place brought you water from the hardest rock; who in this wilderness fed you with manna that your fathers had not known.'

The word of the Lord.
Thanks be to God.

RESPONSORIAL PSALM   *Psalm 147:12–15, 19–20 response v 12*

O praise the Lord, Jerusalem!

or

Alleluia! *(may be repeated two or three times)*

1   O praise the Lord, Jerusalem!
Zion praise your God!
He has strengthened the bars of your gates,
he has blessed the children within you.

2   He established peace on your borders,
he feeds you with finest wheat.
He sends out his word to the earth
and swiftly runs his command.

3   He makes his word known to Jacob
to Israel his laws and decrees.
He has not dealt thus with other nations;
he has not taught them his decrees.

SECOND READING   *1 Corinthians 10:16–17*

That there is only one loaf means that, though there are many of us, we form a single body.

The blessing-cup that we bless is a communion with the blood of Christ, and the bread that we break is a communion with the body of Christ. The fact that there is only one loaf means that, though there are many of us, we form a single body because we all have a share in this one loaf.

The word of the Lord.
Thanks be to God.

SEQUENCE

The sequence may be said or sung in full, or using the shorter form indicated by the asterisked verses

Sing forth, O Zion, sweetly sing
The praises of thy Shepherd-King,
In hymns and canticles divine;
Dare all thou canst, thou hast no song
Worthy his praises to prolong,
So far surpassing powers like thine.

Today no theme of common praise
Forms the sweet burden of thy lays –
The living, life-dispensing food –
That food which at the sacred board
Unto the brethren twelve our Lord
His parting legacy bestowed.

Then be the anthem clear and strong,
Thy fullest-note, thy sweetest song,
The very music of the breast:
For now shines forth the day sublime
That brings remembrance of the time
When Jesus first his table blessed.

Within our new King's banquet-hall
They meet to keep the festival
That closed the ancient paschal rite:
The old is by the new replaced;
The substance hath the shadow chased;
And rising day dispels the night.

Christ willed what he himself had done
Should be renewed while time should run,
In memory of his parting hour:
Thus, tutored in his school divine,
We consecrate the bread and wine;
And lo – a Host of saving power.

This faith to Christian men is given –
Bread is made flesh by words from heaven:
Into his blood the wine is turned:
What though it baffles nature's powers
Of sense and sight? This faith of ours
Proves more than nature e'er discerned.

Concealed beneath the two-fold sign,
Meet symbols of the gifts divine,
There lie the mysteries adored:
The living body is our food;
Our drink the ever-precious blood;
In each, one undivided Lord.

Not he that eateth it divides
The sacred food, which whole abides
Unbroken still, nor knows decay;
Be one, or be a thousand fed,
They eat alike that living bread
Which, still received, ne'er wastes away.

The good, the guilty share therein,
With sure increase of grace or sin,
The ghostly life, or ghostly death:
Death to the guilty; to the good
Immortal life. See how one food
Man's joy or woe accomplisheth.

We break the Sacrament; but bold
And firm thy faith shall keep its hold;
Deem not the whole doth more enfold
Than in the fractured part resides:
Deem not that Christ doth broken lie;
'Tis but the sign that meets the eye;
The hidden deep reality
In all its fullness still abides.

* Behold the bread of angels, sent
For pilgrims in their banishment,
The bread for God's true children meant,
That may not unto dogs be given:
Oft in the olden types foreshowed;
In Isaac on the altar bowed,
And in the ancient paschal food,
And in the manna sent from heaven.

* Come then, good shepherd, bread divine,
Still show to us thy mercy sign;
Oh, feed us still, still keep us thine;
So may we see thy glories shine
In fields of immortality;

* O thou, the wisest, mightiest, best,
Our present food, our future rest,
Come, make us each thy chosen guest,
Co-heirs of thine, and comrades blest
With saints whose dwelling is with thee.

GOSPEL ACCLAMATION   *John 6:51–52*

Alleluia, alleluia!
I am the living bread which has come down from heaven,
says the Lord.
Anyone who eats this bread will live for ever.
Alleluia!

GOSPEL John 6:51–58

The Lord be with you.
And with your spirit.

A reading from the holy Gospel according to John.
Glory to you, O Lord.

My flesh is real food and my blood is real drink.

Jesus said to the Jews:

'I am the living bread which has come down from heaven. Anyone who eats this bread will live for ever; and the bread that I shall give is my flesh, for the life of the world.'

Then the Jews started arguing with one another: 'How can this man give us his flesh to eat?' they said. Jesus replied:

'I tell you most solemnly, if you do not eat the flesh of the Son of Man and drink his blood, you will not have life in you. Anyone who does eat my flesh and drink my blood has eternal life, and I shall raise him up on the last day. For my flesh is real food and my blood is real drink. He who eats my flesh and drinks my blood lives in me and I live in him. As I, who am sent by the living Father, myself draw life from the Father, so whoever eats me will draw life from me. This is the bread come down from heaven: not like the bread our ancestors ate: they are dead, but anyone who eats this bread will live for ever.'

The Gospel of the Lord.
Praise to you, Lord Jesus Christ.

▷ *page 11*

PRAYER OVER THE OFFERINGS

Grant your Church, O Lord, we pray,
the gifts of unity and peace,
whose signs are to be seen in mystery
in the offerings we here present.
Through Christ our Lord. **Amen.**

▷ *page 15*

Preface II or I of the Most Holy Eucharist, page 65.

COMMUNION ANTIPHON John 6:57

Whoever eats my flesh and drinks my blood
remains in me and I in him, says the Lord.

▷ *page 58*

PRAYER AFTER COMMUNION

Grant, O Lord, we pray,
that we may delight for all eternity
in that share in your divine life,
which is foreshadowed in the present age
by our reception of your precious Body and Blood.
Who live and reign for ever and ever. **Amen.**

PROCESSION

It is desirable that a procession take place after the Mass in which the Host to be carried in the procession is consecrated. However, nothing prohibits a procession from taking place even after a public and lengthy period of adoration following the Mass. If a procession takes place after Mass, when the Communion of the faithful is over, the monstrance in which the consecrated host has been placed is set on the altar. When the Prayer after Communion has been said, the Concluding Rites are omitted and the procession forms.

If there is no procession (▷ *page 59*)

MOST SACRED HEART OF JESUS

FRIDAY AFTER THE SECOND SUNDAY AFTER PENTECOST

ENTRANCE ANTIPHON   *Psalm 32:11, 19*

The designs of his Heart are from age to age,
to rescue their souls from death,
and to keep them alive in famine.   (▷ *page 7*)

The Gloria is sung (said).

COLLECT

Grant, we pray, almighty God,
that we, who glory in the Heart of your beloved Son
and recall the wonders of his love for us,
may be made worthy to receive
an overflowing measure of grace
from that fount of heavenly gifts.
Through our Lord Jesus Christ, your Son,
who lives and reigns with you in the unity of the Holy Spirit,
one God, for ever and ever. **Amen.**
or
O God, who in the Heart of your Son,
wounded by our sins,
bestow on us in mercy
the boundless treasures of your love,
grant, we pray,
that, in paying him the homage of our devotion,
we may also offer worthy reparation.
Through our Lord Jesus Christ, your Son,
who lives and reigns with you in the unity of the Holy Spirit,
one God, for ever and ever. **Amen.**

FIRST READING   *Deuteronomy 7:6–11*

The Lord set his heart on you and chose you.

Moses said to the people: 'You are a people consecrated to the Lord your God; it is you that the Lord our God has chosen to be his very own people out of all the peoples on the earth.

'If the Lord set his heart on you and chose you, it was not because you outnumbered other peoples: you were the least of all peoples. It was for love of you and to keep the oath he swore to your fathers that the Lord brought you out with his mighty hand and redeemed you from the house of slavery, from the power of Pharaoh king of Egypt. Know then that the Lord your God is God indeed, the faithful God who is true to his covenant and his graciousness for a thousand generations towards those who love him and keep his commandments, but who punishes in their own persons those that hate him; he makes him work out his punishment in person. You are therefore to keep and observe the commandments and statutes and ordinances that I lay down for you today.'

The word of the Lord.
Thanks be to God.

RESPONSORIAL PSALM   *Psalm 102:1–4, 6–8, 10 response v 17*

The love of the Lord is everlasting upon those who hold him in fear.

1   My soul, give thanks to the Lord,
all my being, bless his holy name.
My soul, give thanks to the Lord
and never forget all his blessings.

2   It is he who forgives all your guilt,
who heals every one of your ills,
who redeems your life from the grave,
who crowns you with love and compassion.

3   The Lord does deeds of justice,
gives judgement for all who are oppressed.
He made known his ways to Moses
and his deeds to Israel's sons.

4   The Lord is compassion and love,
slow to anger and rich in mercy.
He does not treat us according to our sins
nor repay us according to our faults.

SECOND READING   *1 John 4:7–16*

Love comes from God.

My dear people, let us love one another since love comes from God and everyone who loves is begotten by God and knows God. Anyone who fails to love can never have known God, because God is love. God's love for us was revealed when God sent into the world his only Son so that we could have life through him; this is the love I mean: not our love for God, but God's love for us when he sent his Son to be the sacrifice that takes our sins away. My dear people, since God has loved us so much, we too should love one another. No one has ever seen God; but as long as we love one another God will live in us and his love will be complete in us. We can know that we are living in him and he is living in us because he lets us share his Spirit. We ourselves saw and we testify that the Father sent his Son as saviour of the world. If anyone acknowledges that Jesus is the Son of God, God lives in him, and he in God. We ourselves have known and put our faith in God's love towards ourselves. God is love and anyone who lives in love lives in God, and God lives in him.

The word of the Lord.
Thanks be to God.

ORDINARY

GOSPEL ACCLAMATION   *Matthew 11:29*

Alleluia, alleluia!
Shoulder my yoke and learn from me
for I am gentle and humble in heart.
Alleluia!

GOSPEL   *Matthew 11:25–30*

The Lord be with you.
And with your spirit.

A reading from the holy Gospel according to Matthew.
Glory to you, O Lord.

I am gentle and humble in heart.

Jesus exclaimed, 'I bless you, Father, Lord of heaven and of earth, for hiding these things from the learned and the clever and revealing them to mere children. Yes, Father, for that is what it pleased you to do. Everything has been entrusted to me by my Father; and no one knows the Son except the Father, just as no one knows the Father except the Son and those to whom the Son chooses to reveal him.

'Come to me, all you who labour and are overburdened, and I will give you rest. Shoulder my yoke and learn from me, for I am gentle and humble in heart, and you will find rest for your souls. Yes, my yoke is easy and my burden light.'

The Gospel of the Lord.
Praise to you, Lord Jesus Christ.

▷ *page 11*

PROFESSION OF FAITH
The Profession of Faith is said.

PRAYER OVER THE OFFERINGS
Look, O Lord, we pray, on the surpassing charity
in the Heart of your beloved Son,
that what we offer may be a gift acceptable to you
and an expiation of our offences.
Through Christ our Lord. **Amen.**

▷ *page 15*

PREFACE
THE BOUNDLESS CHARITY OF CHRIST.

Priest: The Lord be with you.
People: **And with your spirit.**

Priest: Lift up your hearts.
People: **We lift them up to the Lord.**

Priest: Let us give thanks to the Lord our God.
People: **It is right and just.**

It is truly right and just, our duty and our salvation,
always and everywhere to give you thanks,
Lord, holy Father, almighty and eternal God,
through Christ our Lord.

For raised up high on the Cross,
he gave himself up for us with a wonderful love
and poured out blood and water from his pierced side,
the wellspring of the Church's Sacraments,
so that, won over to the open heart of the Saviour,
all might draw water joyfully from the springs of salvation.

And so, with all the Angels and Saints,
we praise you, as without end we acclaim:

Holy, Holy, Holy Lord God of hosts...

COMMUNION ANTIPHON   cf John 7:37–38
Thus says the Lord:
Let whoever is thirsty come to me and drink.
Streams of living water will flow
from within the one who believes in me.
or   John 19:34
One of the soldiers opened his side with a lance,
and at once there came forth blood and water.

▷ page 58

PRAYER AFTER COMMUNION
May this sacrament of charity, O Lord,
make us fervent with the fire of holy love,
so that, drawn always to your Son,
we may learn to see him in our neighbour.
Through Christ our Lord.   **Amen.**

▷ page 59

ELEVENTH SUNDAY IN ORDINARY TIME

ENTRANCE ANTIPHON *cf Psalm 26:7, 9*
O Lord, hear my voice, for I have called to you; be my help.
Do not abandon or forsake me, O God, my Saviour! ▷ *page 7*

COLLECT
O God, strength of those who hope in you,
graciously hear our pleas,
and, since without you mortal frailty can do nothing,
grant us always the help of your grace,
that in following your commands
we may please you by our resolve and our deeds.
Through our Lord Jesus Christ, your Son,
who lives and reigns with you in the unity of the Holy Spirit,
one God, for ever and ever. **Amen.**

FIRST READING *Exodus 19:2–6*
I will count you a kingdom of priests, a consecrated nation.

From Rephidim the Israelites set out again; and when they reached the wilderness of Sinai, there in the wilderness they pitched their camp; there facing the mountain Israel pitched camp.

Moses then went up to God, and the Lord called to him from the mountain, saying, 'Say this to the House of Jacob, declare this to the sons of Israel, "You yourselves have seen what I did with the Egyptians, how I carried you on eagle's wings and brought you to myself. From this you know that now, if you obey my voice and hold fast to my covenant, you of all the nations shall be my very own for all the earth is mine. I will count you a kingdom of priests, a consecrated nation."'

The word of the Lord.
Thanks be to God.

RESPONSORIAL PSALM *Psalm 99:1–3, 5 response v 3*

**We are his people,
the sheep of his flock.**

1 Cry out with joy to the Lord, all the earth.
Serve the Lord with gladness.
Come before him, singing for joy.

2 Know that he, the Lord, is God.
He made us, we belong to him,
we are his people, the sheep of his flock.

3 Indeed, how good is the Lord,
eternal his merciful love.
He is faithful from age to age.

SECOND READING *Romans 5:6–11*

Now that we have been reconciled by the death of his Son, surely we may count on being saved by the life of his Son.

We were still helpless when at his appointed moment Christ died for sinful men. It is not easy to die even for a good man – though of course for someone really worthy, a man might be prepared to die – but what proves that God loves us is that Christ died for us while we were still sinners. Having died to make us righteous, is it likely that he would now fail to save us from God's anger? When we were reconciled to God by the death of his Son, we were still enemies; now that we have been reconciled, surely we may count on being saved by the life of his Son? Not merely because we have been reconciled but because we are filled with joyful trust in God through our Lord Jesus Christ, through whom we have already gained our reconciliation.

The word of the Lord.
Thanks be to God.

GOSPEL ACCLAMATION *John 10:27*

Alleluia, alleluia!
The sheep that belong to me listen to my voice,
says the Lord,
I know them and they follow me.
Alleluia!

or *Mark 1:15*

Alleluia, alleluia!
The kingdom of God is close at hand.
Repent, and believe the Good News.
Alleluia!

GOSPEL *Matthew: 9:36–10:8*

The Lord be with you.
And with your spirit.

A reading from the holy Gospel according to Matthew.
Glory to you, O Lord.

He summoned his twelve disciples, and sent them out.

When Jesus saw the crowds he felt sorry for them because they were harassed and dejected, like sheep without a shepherd. Then he said to his disciples, 'The harvest is rich but the labourers are few, so ask the Lord of the harvest to send labourers to his harvest.'

He summoned his twelve disciples, and gave them authority over unclean spirits with power to cast them out and to cure all kinds of diseases and sickness.

These are the names of the twelve apostles: first, Simon who is called Peter, and his brother Andrew; James the son of Zebedee, and his brother John; Philip and Bartholomew; Thomas, and Matthew the tax collector; James the son of Alphaeus, and Thaddaeus; Simon the Zealot and Judas Iscariot, the one who was to betray him. These twelve Jesus sent out, instructing them as follows:

'Do not turn your steps to pagan territory, and do not enter any Samaritan town; go rather to the lost sheep of the House of Israel. And as you go, proclaim that the kingdom of heaven is close at hand.

Cure the sick, raise the dead, cleanse the lepers, cast out devils. You received without charge, give without charge.'

The Gospel of the Lord.
Praise to you, Lord Jesus Christ.

▷ *page 11*

PRAYER OVER THE OFFERINGS

O God, who in the offerings presented here
provide for the twofold needs of human nature,
nourishing us with food
and renewing us with your Sacrament,
grant, we pray,
that the sustenance they provide
may not fail us in body or in spirit.
Through Christ our Lord. **Amen.**

▷ *page 15*

COMMUNION ANTIPHON   *Psalm 26:4*

There is one thing I ask of the Lord, only this do I seek:
to live in the house of the Lord all the days of my life.

or   *John 17:11*

Holy Father, keep in your name those you have given me,
that they may be one as we are one, says the Lord.

▷ *page 58*

PRAYER AFTER COMMUNION

As this reception of your Holy Communion, O Lord,
foreshadows the union of the faithful in you,
so may it bring about unity in your Church.
Through Christ our Lord. **Amen.**

▷ *page 59*

TWELFTH SUNDAY IN ORDINARY TIME

ENTRANCE ANTIPHON   *cf Psalm 27:8–9*

The Lord is the strength of his people,
a saving refuge for the one he has anointed.
Save your people, Lord, and bless your heritage,
and govern them for ever.

▷ *page 7*

COLLECT

Grant, O Lord,
that we may always revere and love your holy name,
for you never deprive of your guidance
those you set firm on the foundation of your love.
Through our Lord Jesus Christ, your Son,
who lives and reigns with you in the unity of the Holy Spirit,
one God, for ever and ever.   **Amen.**

FIRST READING   *Jeremiah 20:10–13*

He has delivered the soul of the needy from the hands of evil men.

Jeremiah said:

I hear so many disparaging me, ' "Terror from every side!" Denounce him! Let us denounce him!' All those who used to be my friends watched for my downfall, 'Perhaps he will be seduced into error. Then we will master him and take our revenge!' But the Lord is at my side, a mighty hero; my opponents will stumble, mastered, confounded by their failure; everlasting, unforgettable disgrace will be theirs. But you, Lord of Hosts, you who probe with justice, who scrutinise the loins and heart, let me see the vengeance you will take on them, for I have committed my cause to you. Sing to the Lord, praise the Lord, for he has delivered the soul of the needy from the hands of evil men.'

The word of the Lord.
Thanks be to God.

RESPONSORIAL PSALM   *Psalm 68:8–10, 14, 17, 33–35 response v 14*

In your great love, answer me, O God.

1   It is for you that I suffer taunts,
    that shame covers my face,
    that I have become a stranger to my brothers,
    an alien to my own mother's sons.
    I burn with zeal for your house
    and taunts against you fall on me.

2   This is my prayer to you,
    my prayer for your favour.
    In your great love, answer me, O God,
    with your help that never fails:
    Lord, answer, for your love is kind;
    in your compassion, turn towards me.

3   The poor when they see it will be glad
    and God-seeking hearts will revive;
    for the Lord listens to the needy
    and does not spurn his servants in their chains.
    Let the heavens and the earth give him praise,
    the sea and all its living creatures.

SECOND READING   *Romans 5:12–15*

The gift considerably outweighed the fall.

Sin entered the world through one man, and through sin death, and thus death has spread through the whole human race because everyone has sinned. Sin existed in the world long before the Law was given. There was no law and so no one could be accused of the sin of 'law-breaking', yet death reigned over all from Adam to Moses, even though their sin, unlike that of Adam, was not a matter of breaking a law.

Adam prefigured the One to come, but the gift itself considerably outweighed the fall. If it is certain that through one man's fall so many died, it is even more certain that divine grace, coming through the one man, Jesus Christ, came to so many as an abundant free gift.

The word of the Lord.
Thanks be to God.

GOSPEL ACCLAMATION   *John 1:14, 12*

Alleluia, alleluia!
The Word was made flesh and lived among us;
to all who did accept him
he gave power to become children of God.
Alleluia!

or   *John 15:26, 27*

Alleluia, alleluia!
The Spirit of truth will be my witness;
and you too will be my witnesses.
Alleluia!

GOSPEL   *Matthew 10:26–33*

The Lord be with you.
And with your spirit.

A reading from the holy Gospel according to Matthew.
Glory to you, O Lord.

Do not be afraid of those who kill the body.

Jesus instructed the Twelve as follows: 'Do not be afraid. For everything that is now covered will be uncovered, and everything now hidden will be made clear. What I say to you in the dark, tell in the daylight; what you hear in whispers, proclaim from the housetops.

'Do not be afraid of those who kill the body but cannot kill the soul; fear him rather who can destroy both body and soul in hell. Can you not buy two sparrows for a penny? And yet not one falls to the ground without your Father knowing. Why, every hair on your head has been counted. So there is no need to be afraid; you are worth more than hundreds of sparrows.

'So if anyone declares himself for me in the presence of men, I will declare myself for him in the presence of my Father in heaven. But the one who disowns me in the presence of men, I will disown in the presence of my Father in heaven.'

The Gospel of the Lord.
Praise to you, Lord Jesus Christ.

▷ *page 11*

PRAYER OVER THE OFFERINGS
Receive, O Lord, the sacrifice of conciliation and praise
and grant that, cleansed by its action,
we may make offering of a heart pleasing to you.
Through Christ our Lord.   **Amen.**

▷ *page 15*

COMMUNION ANTIPHON   *Psalm 144:15*
The eyes of all look to you, Lord,
and you give them their food in due season.

or   John 10:11, 15

I am the Good Shepherd,
and I lay down my life for my sheep, says the Lord.

▷ *page 58*

PRAYER AFTER COMMUNION
Renewed and nourished
by the Sacred Body and Precious Blood of your Son,
we ask of your mercy, O Lord,
that what we celebrate with constant devotion
may be our sure pledge of redemption.
Through Christ our Lord.   **Amen.**

▷ *page 59*

THIRTEENTH SUNDAY IN ORDINARY TIME

ENTRANCE ANTIPHON   *Psalm 46:2*
All peoples, clap your hands.
Cry to God with shouts of joy!

▷ *page 7*

COLLECT
O God, who through the grace of adoption
chose us to be children of light,
grant, we pray,
that we may not be wrapped in the darkness of error
but always be seen to stand in the bright light of truth.
Through our Lord Jesus Christ, your Son,
who lives and reigns with you in the unity of the Holy Spirit,
one God, for ever and ever.   **Amen.**

FIRST READING   *2 Kings 4:8–11,14–16*
This is a holy man of God; let him rest there.

One day as Elisha was on his way to
Shunem, a woman of rank who lived
there pressed him to stay and eat there.
After this he always broke his journey
for a meal when he passed that way. She
said to her husband, 'Look, I am sure the
man who is constantly passing our way
must be a holy man of God. Let us build
him a small room on the roof, and put
him a bed in it, and a table and chair

and lamp; whenever he comes to us he can rest there.'

One day when he came, he retired to the upper room and lay down. 'What can be done for her?' he asked. Gehazi, his servant, answered, 'Well, she has no son and her husband is old.' Elisha said, 'Call her.' The servant called her and she stood at the door. 'This time next year,' he said, 'you will hold a son in your arms.'

The word of the Lord.

Thanks be to God.

RESPONSORIAL PSALM   *Psalm 88:2–3, 16–19 response v 2*

I will sing for ever of your love, O Lord.

1   I will sing for ever of your love, O Lord;
    through all ages my mouth will proclaim your truth.
    Of this I am sure, that your love lasts for ever,
    that your truth is firmly established as the heavens.

2   Happy the people who acclaim such a king,
    who walk, O Lord, in the light of your face,
    who find their joy every day in your name,
    who make your justice the source of their bliss.

3   For it is you, O Lord, who are the glory of their strength;
    it is by your favour that our might is exalted:
    for our ruler is in the keeping of the Lord;
    our king in the keeping of the Holy One of Israel.

SECOND READING   *Romans 6:3–4, 8–11*

When we were baptised we went into the tomb with Christ, so that we too might live a new life.

When we were baptised in Christ Jesus we were baptised in his death; in other words, when we were baptised we went into the tomb with him and joined him in death, so that as Christ was raised from the dead by the Father's glory, we too might live a new life.

But we believe that having died with Christ we shall return to life with him: Christ, as we know, having been raised from the dead will never die again. Death has no power over him any more. When he died, he died, once for all, to sin, so his life now is life with God; and in that way, you too must consider yourselves to be dead to sin but alive for God in Christ Jesus.

The word of the Lord.

Thanks be to God.

ORDINARY

GOSPEL ACCLAMATION   *cf Acts 16:14*

Alleluia, alleluia!
Open our heart, O Lord,
to accept the words of your Son.
Alleluia!

or   *1 Peter 2:9*

Alleluia, alleluia!
You are a chosen race, a royal priesthood, a people set apart
to sing the praises of God
who called you out of darkness into his wonderful light.
Alleluia!

GOSPEL   *Matthew 10:37–42*

The Lord be with you.
And with your spirit.

A reading from the holy Gospel according to Matthew.
Glory to you, O Lord.

Anyone who does not take his cross is not worthy of me. Anyone who welcomes you welcomes me.

Jesus instructed the Twelve as follows: 'Anyone who prefers father or mother to me is not worthy of me. Anyone who prefers son or daughter to me is not worthy of me. Anyone who does not take his cross and follow in my footsteps is not worthy of me. Anyone who finds his life will lose it; anyone who loses his life for my sake will find it.

'Anyone who welcomes you welcomes me; and those who welcome me welcome the one who sent me.

'Anyone who welcomes a prophet because he is a prophet will have a prophet's reward; and anyone who welcomes a holy man because he is a holy man will have a holy man's reward.

'If anyone gives so much as a cup of cold water to one of these little ones because he is a disciple, then I tell you solemnly, he will most certainly not lose his reward.'

The Gospel of the Lord.
Praise to you, Lord Jesus Christ.

▷ *page 11*

PRAYER OVER THE OFFERINGS
O God, who graciously accomplish
the effects of your mysteries,
grant, we pray,
that the deeds by which we serve you
may be worthy of these sacred gifts.
Through Christ our Lord.   **Amen.**

▷ *page 15*

COMMUNION ANTIPHON   *cf Psalm 102:1*

Bless the Lord, O my soul,
and all within me, his holy name.

or   *John 17:20–21*

O Father, I pray for them, that they may be one in us,
that the world may believe that you have sent me, says the Lord.

▷ *page 58*

PRAYER AFTER COMMUNION

May this divine sacrifice we have offered and received
fill us with life, O Lord, we pray,
so that, bound to you in lasting charity,
we may bear fruit that lasts for ever.
Through Christ our Lord.   **Amen.**

▷ *page 59*

ORDINARY

FOURTEENTH SUNDAY IN ORDINARY TIME

ENTRANCE ANTIPHON   *cf Psalm 47:10–11*

Your merciful love, O God,
we have received in the midst of your temple.
Your praise, O God, like your name,
reaches the ends of the earth;
your right hand is filled with saving justice.

▷ *page 7*

COLLECT

O God, who in the abasement of your Son
have raised up a fallen world,
fill your faithful with holy joy,
for on those you have rescued from slavery to sin
you bestow eternal gladness.
Through our Lord Jesus Christ, your Son,
who lives and reigns with you in the unity of the Holy Spirit,
one God, for ever and ever.   **Amen.**

FIRST READING   *Zechariah 9:9–10*

See now, your king comes humbly to you.

The Lord says this:

'Rejoice heart and soul, daughter of Zion! Shout with gladness, daughter of Jerusalem! See now, your king comes to you; he is victorious, he is triumphant, humble and riding on a donkey, on a colt, the foal of a donkey. He will banish chariots from Ephraim and horses from Jerusalem; the bow of war will be banished. He will proclaim peace for the nations. His empire shall stretch from sea to sea, from the River to the ends of the earth.'

The word of the Lord.
Thanks be to God.

RESPONSORIAL PSALM *Psalm 144:1–2, 8–11, 13–14 response v 1*

I will bless your name for ever, O God my King.

or

Alleluia! *(may be repeated two or three times)*

1 I will give you glory, O God my King,
   I will bless your name for ever.
   I will bless you day after day
   and praise your name for ever.

2 The Lord is kind and full of compassion,
   slow to anger, abounding in love.
   How good is the Lord to all,
   compassionate to all his creatures.

3 All your creatures shall thank you, O Lord,
   and your friends shall repeat their blessing.
   They shall speak of the glory of your reign
   and declare your might, O God.

4 The Lord is faithful in all his words
   and loving in all his deeds.
   The Lord supports all who fall
   and raises all who are bowed down.

SECOND READING *Romans 8:9, 11–13*

If by the Spirit you put an end to the misdeeds of the body, you will live.

Your interests are not in the unspiritual, but in the spiritual, since the Spirit of God has made his home in you. In fact, unless you possessed the Spirit of Christ you would not belong to him, and if the Spirit of him who raised Jesus from the dead is living in you, then he who raised Jesus from the dead will give life to your own mortal bodies through his Spirit living in you.

So then, my brothers, there is no necessity for us to obey our unspiritual selves or to live unspiritual lives. If you do live in that way, you are doomed to die; but if by the Spirit you put an end to the misdeeds of the body you will live.

The word of the Lord.
Thanks be to God.

GOSPEL ACCLAMATION *cf Matthew 11:25*

Alleluia, alleluia!
Blessed are you, Father, Lord of heaven and earth,
for revealing the mysteries of the kingdom to mere children.
Alleluia!

GOSPEL *Matthew 11:25–30*

The Lord be with you.
And with your spirit.

A reading from the holy Gospel according to Matthew.
Glory to you, O Lord.

I am gentle and humble of heart.

Jesus exclaimed, 'I bless you, Father, Lord of heaven and of earth, for hiding these things from the learned and the clever and revealing them to mere children. Yes, Father, for that is what it pleased you to do. Everything has been entrusted to me by my Father; and no one knows the Son except the Father, just as no one knows the Father except the Son and those to whom the Son chooses to reveal him.

'Come to me, all you who labour and are overburdened, and I will give you rest. Shoulder my yoke and learn from me, for I am gentle and humble in heart, and you will find rest for your souls. Yes, my yoke is easy and my burden light.'

The Gospel of the Lord.
Praise to you, Lord Jesus Christ.

▷ *page 11*

PRAYER OVER THE OFFERINGS

May this oblation dedicated to your name
purify us, O Lord,
and day by day bring our conduct
closer to the life of heaven.
Through Christ our Lord. **Amen.**

▷ *page 15*

COMMUNION ANTIPHON *Psalm 33:9*

Taste and see that the Lord is good;
blessed the man who seeks refuge in him.

or *Matthew 11:28*

Come to me, all who labour and are burdened,
and I will refresh you, says the Lord.

▷ *page 58*

PRAYER AFTER COMMUNION

Grant, we pray, O Lord,
that, having been replenished by such great gifts,
we may gain the prize of salvation
and never cease to praise you.
Through Christ our Lord. **Amen.**

▷ *page 59*

ORDINARY

✠ FIFTEENTH SUNDAY IN ORDINARY TIME

ENTRANCE ANTIPHON *cf Psalm 16:15*

As for me, in justice I shall behold your face;
I shall be filled with the vision of your glory.

▷ *page 7*

COLLECT

O God, who show the light of your truth
to those who go astray,
so that they may return to the right path,
give all who for the faith they profess
are accounted Christians
the grace to reject whatever is contrary to the name of Christ
and to strive after all that does it honour.
Through our Lord Jesus Christ, your Son,
who lives and reigns with you in the unity of the Holy Spirit,
one God, for ever and ever. **Amen.**

FIRST READING *Isaiah 55:10–11*

The rain makes the earth give growth.

Thus says the Lord: 'As the rain and the snow come down from the heavens and do not return without watering the earth, making it yield and giving growth to provide seed for the sower and bread for the eating, so the word that goes from my mouth does not return to me empty, without carrying out my will and succeeding in what it was sent to do.'

The word of the Lord.
Thanks be to God.

RESPONSORIAL PSALM *Psalm 64:10–14 response Luke 8:8*

**Some seed fell into rich soil,
and produced its crop.**

1   You care for the earth, give it water,
    you fill it with riches.
    Your river in heaven brims over
    to provide its grain.

2   And thus you provide for the earth;
    you drench its furrows,
    you level it, soften it with showers,
    you bless its growth.

3   You crown the year with your goodness.
    Abundance flows in your steps,
    in the pastures of the wilderness it flows.

4   The hills are girded with joy,
    the meadows covered with flocks
    the valleys are decked with wheat.
    They shout for joy, yes, they sing.

SECOND READING   Romans 8:18–23
The whole creation is eagerly waiting for God to reveal his sons.

I think that what we suffer in this life can never be compared to the glory, as yet unrevealed, which is waiting for us. The whole creation is eagerly waiting for God to reveal his sons. It was not for any fault on the part of creation that it was made unable to attain its purpose, it was made so by God; but creation still retains the hope of being freed, like us, from its slavery to decadence, to enjoy the same freedom and glory as the children of God. From the beginning till now the entire creation, as we know, has been groaning in one great act of giving birth; and not only creation, but all of us who possess the first-fruits of the Spirit, we too groan inwardly as we wait for our bodies to be set free.

The word of the Lord.
Thanks be to God.

ORDINARY

GOSPEL ACCLAMATION   I Samuel 3:9, John 6:68

Alleluia, alleluia!
Speak, Lord, your servant is listening;
you have the message of eternal life.
Alleluia!

or

Alleluia, alleluia!
The seed is the word of God, Christ the sower;
whoever finds this seed will remain for ever.
Alleluia!

GOSPEL   Matthew 13:1–23   Shorter form (omitting oblique text): Matthew 13:1–9

The Lord be with you.
And with your spirit.

A reading from the holy Gospel according to Matthew.
Glory to you, O Lord.

A sower went out to sow.

Jesus left the house and sat by the lakeside, but such crowds gathered round him that he got into a boat and sat there. The people all stood on the beach, and he told them many things in parables.

He said, 'Imagine a sower going out to sow. As he sowed, some seeds fell on the edge of the path, and the birds came and ate them up. Others fell on patches of rock where they found little soil and sprang up straight away, because there was no depth of earth; but as soon as the sun came up they were scorched and, not having any roots, they withered away. Others fell among thorns, and the thorns grew up and choked them. Others fell on rich soil and produced their crop, some a hundredfold, some sixty, some thirty. Listen, anyone who has ears!'

Then the disciples went up to him and asked, 'Why do you talk to them in parables?' 'Because,' he replied, 'the mysteries of the kingdom of heaven are revealed to you, but they are not revealed to them. For anyone who has will be given more, and he will have more than enough; but from anyone who has not, even what he has will be taken away. The reason I talk to them in parables is that they look without seeing and listen without hearing or understanding. So in their case this prophecy of Isaiah is being fulfilled:

You will listen and listen again, but not understand, see and see again, but not perceive. For the heart of this nation has grown coarse, their ears are dull of hearing, and they have shut their eyes, for fear they should see with their eyes, hear with their ears, understand with their heart, and be converted and be healed by me.

But happy are your eyes because they see, your ears because they hear! I tell you solemnly, many prophets and holy men longed to see what you see, and never saw it; to hear what you hear, and never heard it.

You, therefore, are to hear the parable of the sower. When anyone hears the word of the kingdom without understanding, the evil one comes and carries off what was sown in his heart: this is the man who received the seed on the edge of the path. The one who received it on patches of rock is the man who hears the word and welcomes it at once with joy. But he has no root in him, he does not last; let some trial come, or some persecution on account of the word, and he falls away at once. The one who received the seed in thorns is the man who hears the word but the worries of this world and the lure of riches choke the word and so he produces nothing. And the one who received the seed in rich soil is the man who hears the word and understands it; he is the one who yields a harvest and produces now a hundredfold, now sixty, now thirty.'

The Gospel of the Lord.
Praise to you, Lord Jesus Christ.

▷ page 11

PRAYER OVER THE OFFERINGS

Look upon the offerings of the Church, O Lord,
as she makes her prayer to you,
and grant that, when consumed by those who believe,
they may bring ever greater holiness.
Through Christ our Lord.   **Amen.**

▷ page 15

COMMUNION ANTIPHON   cf Psalm 83:4–5

The sparrow finds a home,
and the swallow a nest for her young:
by your altars, O Lord of hosts, my King and my God.
Blessed are they who dwell in your house,
for ever singing your praise.

or   John 6:57

Whoever eats my flesh and drinks my blood
remains in me and I in him, says the Lord.

▷ page 58

PRAYER AFTER COMMUNION

Having consumed these gifts, we pray, O Lord,
that, by our participation in this mystery,
its saving effects upon us may grow.
Through Christ our Lord. **Amen.**

▷ *page 59*

SIXTEENTH SUNDAY IN ORDINARY TIME

ENTRANCE ANTIPHON *Psalm 53:6, 8*

See, I have God for my help.
The Lord sustains my soul.
I will sacrifice to you with willing heart,
and praise your name, O Lord, for it is good.

▷ *page 7*

COLLECT

Show favour, O Lord, to your servants
and mercifully increase the gifts of your grace,
that, made fervent in hope, faith and charity,
they may be ever watchful in keeping your commands.
Through our Lord Jesus Christ, your Son,
who lives and reigns with you in the unity of the Holy Spirit,
one God, for ever and ever. **Amen.**

FIRST READING *Wisdom 12:13, 16–19*

After sin you will grant repentance.

There is no god, other than you, who cares for everything, to whom you might have to prove that you never judged unjustly. Your justice has its source in strength, your sovereignty over all makes you lenient to all. You show your strength when your sovereign power is questioned and you expose the insolence of those who know it; but, disposing of such strength, you are mild in judgement, you govern us with great lenience, for you have only to will, and your power is there. By acting thus you have taught a lesson to your people how the virtuous man must be kindly to his fellow men, and you have given your sons the good hope that after sin you will grant repentance.

The word of the Lord.
Thanks be to God.

RESPONSORIAL PSALM *Psalm 85:5–6, 9–10, 15–16 response v 5*

O Lord, you are good and forgiving.

1 O Lord, you are good and forgiving,
   full of love to all who call.
   Give heed, O Lord, to my prayer
   and attend to the sound of my voice.

continued...

O Lord, you are good and forgiving.

2   All the nations shall come to adore you
    and glorify your name, O Lord:
    for you are great and do marvellous deeds,
    you who alone are God.

3   But you, God of mercy and compassion,
    slow to anger, O Lord,
    abounding in love and truth,
    turn and take pity on me.

SECOND READING   *Romans 8:26–27*

The Spirit expresses our plea in a way that could never be put into words.

The Spirit comes to help us in our weakness. For when we cannot choose words in order to pray properly, the Spirit himself expresses our plea in a way that could never be put into words, and God who knows everything in our hearts knows perfectly well what he means, and that the pleas of the saints expressed by the Spirit are according to the mind of God.

The word of the Lord.
Thanks be to God.

GOSPEL ACCLAMATION   *Ephesians 1:17, 18*

Alleluia, alleluia!
May the Father of our Lord Jesus Christ
enlighten the eyes of our mind,
so that we can see what hope his call holds for us.
Alleluia!

or   *Matthew 11:25*

Alleluia, alleluia!
Blessed are you, Father,
Lord of heaven and earth,
for revealing the mysteries of the kingdom
to mere children.
Alleluia!

GOSPEL   *Matthew 13:24–43   Shorter form (omitting oblique text): Matthew 13:24–30*

The Lord be with you.
And with your spirit.

A reading from the holy Gospel according to Matthew.
Glory to you, O Lord.

Let them both grow till the harvest.

Jesus put a parable before the crowds, 'The kingdom of heaven may be compared to a man who sowed good seed in his field. While everybody was asleep his enemy came, sowed darnel all among the wheat, and made off. When the new wheat sprouted and ripened, the darnel appeared as well. The owner's servants went to him and said, "Sir, was it not good seed that you sowed in your field? If so, where does the darnel come from?" "Some enemy has done this," he answered. And the servants said, "Do you want us to go and weed it out?" But he said, "No, because when you weed out the darnel you might pull up the wheat with it. Let them both grow till the harvest; and at harvest time I shall say to the reapers: First collect the darnel and tie it in bundles to be burnt, then gather the wheat into my barn."'

He put another parable before them, 'The kingdom of heaven is like a mustard seed which a man took and sowed in his field. It is the smallest of all the seeds, but when it has grown it is the biggest shrub of all and becomes a tree so that the birds of the air come and shelter in its branches.'

He told them another parable, 'The kingdom of heaven is like the yeast a woman took and mixed in with three measures of flour till it was leavened all through.'

In all this Jesus spoke to the crowds in parables; indeed, he would never speak to them except in parables. This was to fulfil the prophecy:

I will speak to you in parables and expound things hidden since the foundation of the world.

Then, leaving the crowds, he went to the house; and his disciples came to him and said, 'Explain the parable about the darnel in the field to us.' He said in reply, 'The sower of the good seed is the Son of Man. The field is the world; the good seed is the subjects of the kingdom; the darnel, the subjects of the evil one; the enemy who sowed them, the devil; the harvest is the end of the world; the reapers are the angels. Well then, just as the darnel is gathered up and burnt in the fire, so it will be at the end of time. The Son of Man will send his angels and they will gather out of his kingdom all things that provoke offences and all who do evil, and throw them into the blazing furnace, where there will be weeping and grinding of teeth. Then the virtuous will shine like the sun in the kingdom of their Father. Listen, anyone who has ears!'

The Gospel of the Lord.
Praise to you, Lord Jesus Christ.

▷ *page 11*

ORDINARY

PRAYER OVER THE OFFERINGS

O God, who in the one perfect sacrifice
brought to completion varied offerings of the law,
accept, we pray, this sacrifice from your faithful servants
and make it holy, as you blessed the gifts of Abel,
so that what each has offered to the honour of your majesty
may benefit the salvation of all.
Through Christ our Lord. **Amen.**

▷ *page 15*

COMMUNION ANTIPHON   *Psalm 110:4–5*

The Lord, the gracious, the merciful,
has made a memorial of his wonders;
he gives food to those who fear him.

or   *Revelation 3:20*

Behold, I stand at the door and knock, says the Lord.
If anyone hears my voice and opens the door to me,
I will enter his house and dine with him, and he with me.

▷ *page 58*

PRAYER AFTER COMMUNION

Graciously be present to your people, we pray, O Lord,
and lead those you have imbued with heavenly mysteries
to pass from former ways to newness of life.
Through Christ our Lord.   **Amen.**

▷ *page 59*

 # SEVENTEENTH SUNDAY IN ORDINARY TIME

ENTRANCE ANTIPHON   *cf Psalm 67:6–7, 36*

God is in his holy place,
God who unites those who dwell in his house;
he himself gives might and strength to his people.

▷ *page 7*

COLLECT

O God, protector of those who hope in you,
without whom nothing has firm foundation, nothing is holy,
bestow in abundance your mercy upon us
and grant that, with you as our ruler and guide,
we may use the good things that pass
in such a way as to hold fast even now
to those that ever endure.
Through our Lord Jesus Christ, your Son,
who lives and reigns with you in the unity of the Holy Spirit,
one God, for ever and ever.   **Amen.**

FIRST READING   *1 Kings 3:5, 7–12*

You have asked for a discerning judgement for yourself.

The Lord appeared to Solomon in a dream and said, 'Ask what you would like me to give you.' Solomon replied, 'Lord, my God, you have made your servant king in succession to David my father. But I am a very young man, unskilled in leadership. Your servant finds himself in the midst of this people of yours that you have chosen, a people so many its numbers cannot be counted or reckoned. Give your servant a heart to understand how to discern between good and evil, for who could govern this people of yours that is so great?' It pleased the Lord that Solomon should have asked for this. 'Since you have asked for this,' the Lord said, 'and not asked for long life for yourself or riches or the lives of your enemies, but have asked for a discerning judgement for yourself, here and now I do what you ask. I give you a heart wise and shrewd as none before you has had and none will have after you.'

The word of the Lord.

Thanks be to God.

RESPONSORIAL PSALM   *Psalm 118:57, 72, 76–77, 127–130 response v 97*

Lord, how I love your law!

1   My part, I have resolved, O Lord,
     is to obey your word.
     The law from your mouth means more to me
     than silver and gold.

2   Let your love be ready to console me
     by your promise to your servant.
     Let your love come to me and I shall live,
     for your law is my delight.

3   That is why I love your commands
     more than finest gold.
     That is why I rule my life by your precepts:
     I hate false ways.

4   Your will is wonderful indeed;
     therefore I obey it.
     The unfolding of your word gives light
     and teaches the simple.

SECOND READING   *Romans 8:28–30*

God intended us to become true images of his Son.

We know that by turning everything to their good God co-operates with all those who love him, with all those that he has called according to his purpose. They are the ones he chose specially long ago and intended to become true images of his Son, so that his Son might be the eldest of many brothers. He called those he intended for this; those he called he justified, and with those he justified he shared his glory.

The word of the Lord.

Thanks be to God.

GOSPEL ACCLAMATION   *John 15:15*

> Alleluia, alleluia!
> I call you friends, says the Lord,
> because I have made known to you
> everything I have learnt from my Father.
> Alleluia!

or   *cf Matthew 11:25*

> Alleluia, alleluia!
> Blessed are you, Father, Lord of heaven and earth,
> for revealing the mysteries of the kingdom
> to mere children.
> Alleluia!

GOSPEL   *Matthew 13:44–52   Shorter form (omitting oblique text): Matthew 13:44–46*

The Lord be with you.
And with your spirit.

A reading from the holy Gospel according to Matthew.
Glory to you, O Lord.

He sells everything he owns and buys the field.

Jesus said to the crowds, 'The kingdom of heaven is like treasure hidden in a field which someone has found; he hides it again, goes off happy, sells everything he owns and buys the field.

'Again, the kingdom of heaven is like a merchant looking for fine pearls; when he finds one of great value he goes and sells everything he owns and buys it.

'Again, the kingdom of heaven is like a dragnet cast into the sea that brings in a haul of all kinds. When it is full, the fishermen haul it ashore; then, sitting down, they collect the good ones in a basket and throw away those that are no use. This is how it will be at the end of time: the angels will appear and separate the wicked from the just to throw them into the blazing furnace where there will be weeping and grinding of teeth.

'Have you understood all this?' They said, 'Yes.' And he said to them, 'Well, then, every scribe who becomes a disciple of the kingdom of heaven is like a householder who brings out from his storeroom things both new and old.'

The Gospel of the Lord.
Praise to you, Lord Jesus Christ.

▷ *page 11*

PRAYER OVER THE OFFERINGS

Accept, O Lord, we pray, the offerings
which we bring from the abundance of your gifts,
that through the powerful working of your grace
these most sacred mysteries may sanctify our present way of life
and lead us to eternal gladness.
Through Christ our Lord.   **Amen.**

▷ *page 15*

COMMUNION ANTIPHON   *Psalm 102:2*

Bless the Lord, O my soul,
and never forget all his benefits.

or   *Matthew 5:7–8*

Blessed are the merciful, for they shall receive mercy.
Blessed are the clean of heart, for they shall see God.

▷ *page 58*

PRAYER AFTER COMMUNION

We have consumed, O Lord, this divine Sacrament,
the perpetual memorial of the Passion of your Son;
grant, we pray, that this gift,
which he himself gave us with love beyond all telling,
may profit us for salvation.
Through Christ our Lord. **Amen.**

▷ *page 59*

ORDINARY

EIGHTEENTH SUNDAY IN ORDINARY TIME

ENTRANCE ANTIPHON   *Psalm 69:2, 6*

O God, come to my assistance;
O Lord, make haste to help me!
You are my rescuer, my help;
O Lord, do not delay.

▷ *page 7*

COLLECT

Draw near to your servants, O Lord,
and answer their prayers with unceasing kindness,
that, for those who glory in you as their Creator and guide,
you may restore what you have created
and keep safe what you have restored.
Through our Lord Jesus Christ, your Son,
who lives and reigns with you in the unity of the Holy Spirit,
one God, for ever and ever. **Amen.**

FIRST READING   *Isaiah 55:1–3*

Come and eat.

Thus says the Lord:

Oh, come to the water all you who are thirsty; though you have no money, come! Buy corn without money, and eat, and, at no cost, wine and milk. Why spend money on what is not bread, your wages on what fails to satisfy? Listen, listen to me and you will have good things to eat and rich food to enjoy. Pay attention, come to me; listen, and your soul will live. With you I will make an everlasting covenant out of the favours promised to David.

The word of the Lord.
Thanks be to God.

RESPONSORIAL PSALM   *Psalm 144:8–9, 15–18 response v 16*

**You open wide your hand, O Lord,
you grant our desires.**

1   The Lord is kind and full of compassion,
slow to anger, abounding in love.
How good is the Lord to all,
compassionate to all his creatures.

2   The eyes of all creatures look to you
and you give them their food in due time.
You open wide your hand,
grant the desires of all who live.

3   The Lord is just in all his ways
and loving in all his deeds.
He is close to all who call him,
call on him from their hearts.

SECOND READING   *Romans 8:35, 37–39*

No created thing can ever come between us and the love of God made visible in Christ.

Nothing can come between us and the love of Christ, even if we are troubled or worried, or being persecuted, or lacking food or clothes, or being threatened or even attacked. These are the trials through which we triumph, by the power of him who loved us.

For I am certain of this: neither death nor life, no angel, no prince, nothing that exists, nothing still to come, not any power, or height or depth, nor any created thing, can ever come between us and the love of God made visible in Christ Jesus our Lord.

The word of the Lord.
Thanks be to God.

GOSPEL ACCLAMATION   *Luke 19:38*

**Alleluia, alleluia!
Blessings on the King who comes,
in the name of the Lord!
Peace in heaven
and glory in the highest heavens!
Alleluia!**

or   *Matthew 4:4*

**Alleluia, alleluia!
Man does not live on bread alone,
but on every word that comes from the mouth of God.
Alleluia!**

GOSPEL   *Matthew 14:13–21*

The Lord be with you.
And with your spirit.

A reading from the holy Gospel according to Matthew.
Glory to you, O Lord.

They all ate as much as they wanted.

When Jesus received the news of John the Baptist's death he withdrew by boat to a lonely place where they could be by themselves. But the people heard of this and, leaving the towns, went after him on foot. So as he stepped ashore he saw a large crowd; and he took pity on them and healed their sick.

When evening came, the disciples went to him and said, 'This is a lonely place, and the time has slipped by; so send the people away, and they can go to the villages to buy themselves some food.' Jesus replied, 'There is no need for them to go: give them something to eat yourselves.' But they answered, 'All we have with us is five loaves and two fish.' 'Bring them here to me,' he said. He gave orders that the people were to sit down on the grass; then he took the five loaves and the two fish, raised his eyes to heaven and said the blessing. And breaking the loaves he handed them to his disciples who gave them to the crowds. They all ate as much as they wanted, and they collected the scraps remaining, twelve baskets full. Those who ate numbered about five thousand men, to say nothing of women and children.

The Gospel of the Lord.
Praise to you, Lord Jesus Christ.

▷ *page 11*

PRAYER OVER THE OFFERINGS
Graciously sanctify these gifts, O Lord, we pray,
and, accepting the oblation of this spiritual sacrifice,
make of us an eternal offering to you.
Through Christ our Lord.   **Amen.**

▷ *page 15*

COMMUNION ANTIPHON   *Wisdom 16:20*
You have given us, O Lord, bread from heaven,
endowed with all delights and sweetness in every taste.

or   *John 6:35*

I am the bread of life, says the Lord;
whoever comes to me will not hunger
and whoever believes in me will not thirst.

▷ *page 58*

PRAYER AFTER COMMUNION

Accompany with constant protection, O Lord,
those you renew with these heavenly gifts
and, in your never-failing care for them,
make them worthy of eternal redemption.
Through Christ our Lord.   **Amen.**

▷ *page 59*

NINETEENTH SUNDAY IN ORDINARY TIME

ENTRANCE ANTIPHON   *cf Psalm 73:20, 19, 22, 23*
Look to your covenant, O Lord,
and forget not the life of your poor ones for ever.
Arise, O God, and defend your cause,
and forget not the cries of those who seek you.

▷ *page 7*

COLLECT

Almighty ever-living God,
whom, taught by the Holy Spirit,
we dare to call our Father,
bring, we pray, to perfection in our hearts
the spirit of adoption as your sons and daughters,
that we may merit to enter into the inheritance
which you have promised.
Through our Lord Jesus Christ, your Son,
who lives and reigns with you in the unity of the Holy Spirit,
one God, for ever and ever.   **Amen.**

FIRST READING   *1 Kings 19:9, 11–13*
Stand on the mountain before the Lord.

When Elijah reached Horeb, the mountain of God, he went into the cave and spent the night in it. Then he was told, "Go out and stand on the mountain before the Lord." Then the Lord himself went by. There came a mighty wind, so strong it tore the mountains and shattered the rocks before the Lord. But the Lord was not in the wind. After the wind came an earthquake. But the Lord was not in the earthquake. After the earthquake came a fire. But the Lord was not in the fire. And after the fire there came the sound of a gentle breeze. And when Elijah heard this, he covered his face with his cloak and went out and stood at the entrance of the cave.

The word of the Lord.
Thanks be to God.

RESPONSORIAL PSALM   *Psalm 84:9–14 response v 8*

**Let us see, O Lord, your mercy
and give us your saving help.**

1   I will hear what the Lord God has to say,
     a voice that speaks of peace.
     His help is near for those who fear him
     and his glory will dwell in our land.

2   Mercy and faithfulness have met;
     justice and peace have embraced.
     Faithfulness shall spring from the earth
     and justice look down from heaven.

3   The Lord will make us prosper
     and our earth shall yield its fruit.
     Justice shall march before him
     and peace shall follow his steps.

SECOND READING   *Romans 9:1–5*

I would willingly be condemned if it could help my brothers.

What I want to say is no pretence; I say it in union with Christ – it is the truth – my conscience in union with the Holy Spirit assures me of it too. What I want to say is this: my sorrow is so great, my mental anguish so endless, I would willingly be condemned and be cut off from Christ if it could help my brothers of Israel, my own flesh and blood. They were adopted as sons, they were given the glory and the covenants; the Law and the ritual were drawn up for them, and the promises were made to them. They are descended from the patriarchs and from their flesh and blood came Christ who is above all, God for ever blessed! Amen.

The word of the Lord.
Thanks be to God.

GOSPEL ACCLAMATION   *Luke 19:38*

**Alleluia, alleluia!
Blessings on the King who comes,
in the name of the Lord!
Peace in heaven
and glory in the highest heavens!
Alleluia!**

or   *Psalm 129:5*

**Alleluia, alleluia!
My soul is waiting for the Lord,
I count on his word.
Alleluia!**

ORDINARY

GOSPEL   *Matthew 14:22–33*

The Lord be with you.
And with your spirit.

A reading from the holy Gospel according to Matthew.
Glory to you, O Lord.

Tell me to come to you across the water.

Jesus made the disciples get into the boat and go on ahead to the other side while he would send the crowds away. After sending the crowds away he went up into the hills by himself to pray. When evening came, he was there alone, while the boat, by now far out on the lake, was battling with a heavy sea, for there was a headwind. In the fourth watch of the night he went towards them, walking on the lake, and when the disciples saw him walking on the lake they were terrified. 'It is a ghost,' they said, and cried out in fear. But at once Jesus called out to them, saying, 'Courage! It is I! Do not be afraid.' It was Peter who answered.

'Lord,' he said, 'if it is you, tell me to come to you across the water.' 'Come,' said Jesus. Then Peter got out of the boat and started walking towards Jesus across the water, but as soon as he felt the force of the wind, he took fright and began to sink. 'Lord! Save me!' he cried. Jesus put out his hand at once and held him. 'Man of little faith,' he said, 'why did you doubt?' And as they got into the boat the wind dropped. The men in the boat bowed down before him and said, 'Truly, you are the Son of God.'

The Gospel of the Lord.
Praise to you, Lord Jesus Christ.

▷ *page 11*

PRAYER OVER THE OFFERINGS

Be pleased, O Lord, to accept the offerings of your Church,
for in your mercy you have given them to be offered
and by your power you transform them
into the mystery of our salvation.
Through Christ our Lord.   **Amen.**

▷ *page 15*

COMMUNION ANTIPHON   *Psalm 147:12, 14*

O Jerusalem, glorify the Lord,
who gives you your fill of finest wheat.

or   cf John 6:51

The bread that I will give, says the Lord,
is my flesh for the life of the world.

▷ *page 58*

PRAYER AFTER COMMUNION

May the communion in your Sacrament
that we have consumed, save us, O Lord,
and confirm us in the light of your truth.
Through Christ our Lord. **Amen.**

▷ *page 59*

TWENTIETH SUNDAY IN ORDINARY TIME

ENTRANCE ANTIPHON   *Psalm 83:10–11*

Turn your eyes, O God, our shield;
and look on the face of your anointed one;
one day within your courts
is better than a thousand elsewhere.

▷ *page 7*

COLLECT

O God, who have prepared for those who love you
good things which no eye can see,
fill our hearts, we pray, with the warmth of your love,
so that, loving you in all things and above all things,
we may attain your promises,
which surpass every human desire.
Through our Lord Jesus Christ, your Son,
who lives and reigns with you in the unity of the Holy Spirit,
one God, for ever and ever. **Amen.**

FIRST READING   *Isaiah 56:1, 6–7*

I will bring foreigners to my holy mountain.

Thus says the Lord: Have a care for justice, act with integrity, for soon my salvation will come and my integrity be manifest.

Foreigners who have attached themselves to the Lord to serve him and to love his name and be his servants – all who observe the sabbath, not profaning it, and cling to my covenant – these I will bring to my holy mountain. I will make them joyful in my house of prayer. Their holocausts and their sacrifices will be accepted on my altar, for my house will be called a house of prayer for all the peoples.

The word of the Lord.
Thanks be to God.

RESPONSORIAL PSALM   *Psalm 66:2–3, 5–6, 8 response v 4*

> **Let the peoples praise you, O God;**
> **let all the peoples praise you.**

1   O God, be gracious and bless us
    and let your face shed its light upon us.
    So will your ways be known upon earth
    and all nations learn your saving help.

2   Let the nations be glad and exult
    for you rule the world with justice.
    With fairness you rule the peoples,
    you guide the nations on earth.

3   Let the peoples praise you, O God;
    let all the peoples praise you.
    May God still give us his blessing
    till the ends of the earth revere him.

SECOND READING   *Romans 11:13–15, 29–32*

With Israel, God never takes back his gifts or revokes his choice.

Let me tell you pagans this: I have been sent to the pagans as their apostle, and I am proud of being sent, but the purpose of it is to make my own people envious of you, and in this way save some of them. Since their rejection meant the reconciliation of the world, do you know what their admission will mean? Nothing less than a resurrection from the dead! God never takes back his gifts or revokes his choice.

Just as you changed from being disobedient to God, and now enjoy mercy because of their disobedience, so those who are disobedient now – and only because of the mercy shown to you – will also enjoy mercy eventually. God has imprisoned all men in their own disobedience only to show mercy to all mankind.

The word of the Lord.
Thanks be to God.

GOSPEL ACCLAMATION   *John 10:27*

> **Alleluia, alleluia!**
> **The sheep that belong to me listen to my voice,**
> **says the Lord,**
> **I know them and they follow me.**
> **Alleluia!**

or   *cf Matthew 4:23*

> **Alleluia, alleluia!**
> **Jesus proclaimed the Good News of the kingdom,**
> **and cured all kinds of sickness among the people.**
> **Alleluia!**

GOSPEL   *Matthew 15:21–28*
The Lord be with you.
And with your spirit.

A reading from the holy Gospel according to Matthew.
Glory to you, O Lord.

Woman, you have great faith.

Jesus left Gennesaret and withdrew to the region of Tyre and Sidon. Then out came a Canaanite woman from that district and started shouting, 'Sir, Son of David, take pity on me. My daughter is tormented by a devil.' But he answered her not a word. And his disciples went and pleaded with him. 'Give her what she wants,' they said 'because she is shouting after us.' He said in reply, 'I was sent only to the lost sheep of the House of Israel.' But the woman had come up and was kneeling at his feet. 'Lord,' she said 'help me.' He replied, 'It is not fair to take the children's food and throw it to the house-dogs.' She retorted, 'Ah yes, sir; but even house-dogs can eat the scraps that fall from their master's table.' Then Jesus answered her, 'Woman you have great faith. Let your wish be granted.' And from that moment her daughter was well again.

The Gospel of the Lord.
Praise to you, Lord Jesus Christ.

▷ *page 11*

PRAYER OVER THE OFFERINGS
Receive our oblation, O Lord,
by which is brought about a glorious exchange,
that, by offering what you have given,
we may merit to receive your very self.
Through Christ our Lord.   **Amen.**

▷ *page 15*

COMMUNION ANTIPHON   *Psalm 129:7*
With the Lord there is mercy;
in him is plentiful redemption.

Or John 6:51–52

I am the living bread that came down from heaven, says the Lord.
Whoever eats of this bread will live for ever.

▷ *page 58*

PRAYER AFTER COMMUNION
Made partakers of Christ through these Sacraments,
we humbly implore your mercy, Lord,
that, conformed to his image on earth,
we may merit also to be his coheirs in heaven.
Who lives and reigns for ever and ever.   **Amen.**

▷ *page 59*

ORDINARY

TWENTY-FIRST SUNDAY IN ORDINARY TIME

ENTRANCE ANTIPHON *cf Psalm 85:1–3*

Turn your ear, O Lord, and answer me;
save the servant who trusts in you, my God.
Have mercy on me, O Lord, for I cry to you all the day long.

▷ *page 7*

COLLECT

O God, who cause the minds of the faithful
to unite in a single purpose,
grant your people to love what you command
and to desire what you promise,
that, amid the uncertainties of this world,
our hearts may be fixed on that place
where true gladness is found.
Through our Lord Jesus Christ, your Son,
who lives and reigns with you in the unity of the Holy Spirit,
one God, for ever and ever. **Amen.**

FIRST READING *Isaiah 22:19–23*

I place the key of the House of David upon his shoulder.

Thus says the Lord of hosts to Shebna, the master of the palace:

I dismiss you from your office, I remove you from your post, and the same day I call on my servant Eliakim son of Hilkiah. I invest him with your robe, gird him with your sash, entrust him with your authority; and he shall be a father to the inhabitants of Jerusalem and to the House of Judah. I place the key of the House of David on his shoulder; should he open, no one shall close, should he close, no one shall open. I drive him like a peg into a firm place; he will become a throne of glory for his father's house.

The word of the Lord.
Thanks be to God.

RESPONSORIAL PSALM *Psalm 137:1–3, 6, 8 response v 8*

**Your love, O Lord, is eternal,
discard not the work of your hands.**

1   I thank you, Lord, with all my heart,
    you have heard the words of my mouth.
    Before the angels I will bless you.
    I will adore before your holy temple.

2   I thank you for your faithfulness and love
    which excel all we ever knew of you.
    On the day I called, you answered;
    you increased the strength of my soul.

3   The Lord is high yet he looks on the lowly
and the haughty he knows from afar.
Your love, O Lord, is eternal,
discard not the work of your hands.

SECOND READING   *Romans 11:33–36*

All that exists comes from him; all is by him and for him.

How rich are the depths of God – how deep his wisdom and knowledge – and how impossible to penetrate his motives or understand his methods! Who could ever know the mind of the Lord? Who could ever be his counsellor? Who could ever give him anything or lend him anything? All that exists comes from him; all is by him and for him. To him be glory for ever! Amen.

The word of the Lord.
Thanks be to God.

GOSPEL ACCLAMATION   *2 Corinthians 5:19*

Alleluia, alleluia!
God in Christ was reconciling the world to himself,
and he has entrusted to us the news that they are reconciled.
Alleluia!

or   *Matthew 16:18*

Alleluia, alleluia!
You are Peter
and on this rock I will build my Church.
And the gates of the underworld can never hold out against it.
Alleluia!

GOSPEL   *Matthew 16:13–20*

The Lord be with you.
And with your spirit.

A reading from the holy Gospel according to Matthew.
Glory to you, O Lord.

You are Peter, and I will give you the keys of the kingdom of heaven.

When Jesus came to the region of Caesarea Philippi he put this question to his disciples, 'Who do people say the Son of Man is?' And they said, 'Some say he is John the Baptist, some Elijah, and others Jeremiah or one of the prophets.' 'But you,' he said, 'who do you say I am?' Then Simon Peter spoke up, 'You are the Christ', he said, 'the Son of the living God.' Jesus replied, 'Simon son of Jonah, you are a happy man! Because it was not flesh and blood that revealed this to you but my Father in heaven. So I now say to you: You are Peter and on this rock I will build my Church. And the gates of the underworld can never hold out against it. I will give you the keys of the kingdom of heaven: whatever you bind on earth shall be considered bound in heaven; whatever you loose on earth shall be considered loosed in heaven.' Then he gave the disciples strict orders not to tell anyone that he was the Christ.

The Gospel of the Lord.
Praise to you, Lord Jesus Christ.

▷ *page 11*

PRAYER OVER THE OFFERINGS

O Lord, who gained for yourself a people by adoption
through the one sacrifice offered once for all,
bestow graciously on us, we pray,
the gifts of unity and peace in your Church.
Through Christ our Lord.   **Amen.**

▷ *page 15*

COMMUNION ANTIPHON   *cf Psalm 103:13–15*

The earth is replete with the fruits of your work, O Lord;
you bring forth bread from the earth
and wine to cheer the heart.

or   *cf John 6:54*

Whoever eats my flesh and drinks my blood
has eternal life, says the Lord,
and I will raise him up on the last day.

▷ *page 58*

PRAYER AFTER COMMUNION

Complete within us, O Lord, we pray,
the healing work of your mercy
and graciously perfect and sustain us,
so that in all things we may please you.
Through Christ our Lord.   **Amen.**

▷ *page 59*

TWENTY-SECOND SUNDAY IN ORDINARY TIME

ENTRANCE ANTIPHON   *cf Psalm 85:3, 5*

Have mercy on me, O Lord, for I cry to you all the day long.
O Lord, you are good and forgiving,
full of mercy to all who call to you.

▷ *page 7*

COLLECT

God of might, giver of every good gift,
put into our hearts the love of your name,
so that, by deepening our sense of reverence,
you may nurture in us what is good
and, by your watchful care,
keep safe what you have nurtured.
Through our Lord Jesus Christ, your Son,
who lives and reigns with you in the unity of the Holy Spirit,
one God, for ever and ever.   **Amen.**

FIRST READING *Jeremiah 20:7–9*

The word of the Lord has meant insult for me.

You have seduced me, Lord, and I have let myself be seduced; you have overpowered me: you were the stronger. I am a daily laughing-stock, everybody's butt. Each time I speak the word, I have to howl and proclaim: 'Violence and ruin!' The word of the Lord has meant for me insult, derision, all day long. I used to say, 'I will not think about him, I will not speak in his name any more.' Then there seemed to be a fire burning in my heart, imprisoned in my bones. The effort to restrain it wearied me, I could not bear it.

The word of the Lord.

Thanks be to God.

RESPONSORIAL PSALM *Psalm 62:2–6, 8–9 response v 2*

For you my soul is thirsting, O Lord, my God.

1 O God, you are my God, for you I long;
   for you my soul is thirsting.
   My body pines for you
   like a dry, weary land without water.

2 So I gaze on you in the sanctuary
   to see your strength and your glory.
   For your love is better than life,
   my lips will speak your praise.

3 So I will bless you all my life,
   in your name I will lift up my hands.
   My soul shall be filled as with a banquet,
   my mouth shall praise you with joy.

4 For you have been my help;
   in the shadow of your wings I rejoice.
   My soul clings to you;
   your right hand holds me fast.

SECOND READING *Romans 12:1–2*

Offer your bodies as a living sacrifice.

Think of God's mercy, my brothers, and worship him, I beg you, in a way that is worthy of thinking beings, by offering your living bodies as a holy sacrifice, truly pleasing to God. Do not model yourselves on the behaviour of the world around you, but let your behaviour change, modelled by your new mind. This is the only way to discover the will of God and know what is good, what it is that God wants, what is the perfect thing to do.

The word of the Lord.

Thanks be to God.

ORDINARY

GOSPEL ACCLAMATION   *cf Ephesians 1:17, 18*

> Alleluia, alleluia!
> May the Father of our Lord Jesus Christ
> enlighten the eyes of our mind,
> so that we can see
> what hope his call holds for us.
> Alleluia!

GOSPEL   *Matthew 16:21–27*

The Lord be with you.
And with your spirit.

A reading from the holy Gospel according to Matthew.
Glory to you, O Lord.

If anyone wants to be a follower of mine, let him renounce himself.

Jesus began to make it clear to his disciples that he was destined to go to Jerusalem and suffer grievously at the hands of the elders and chief priests and scribes, to be put to death and to be raised up on the third day. Then, taking him aside, Peter started to remonstrate with him. 'Heaven preserve you, Lord,' he said. 'This must not happen to you.' But he turned and said to Peter, 'Get behind me, Satan! You are an obstacle in my path, because the way you think is not God's way but man's.'

Then Jesus said to his disciples, 'If anyone wants to be a follower of mine, let him renounce himself and take up his cross and follow me. For anyone who wants to save his life will lose it; but anyone who loses his life for my sake will find it. What, then, will a man gain if he wins the whole world and ruins his life? Or what has a man to offer in exchange for his life?

'For the Son of Man is going to come in the glory of his Father with his angels, and, when he does, he will reward each one according to his behaviour.'

The Gospel of the Lord.
Praise to you, Lord Jesus Christ.

▷ *page 11*

PRAYER OVER THE OFFERINGS
May this sacred offering, O Lord,
confer on us always the blessing of salvation,
that what it celebrates in mystery
it may accomplish in power.
Through Christ our Lord.   **Amen.**

▷ *page 15*

COMMUNION ANTIPHON   *Psalm 30:20*

How great is the goodness, Lord,
that you keep for those who fear you.

or   *Matthew 5:9–10*

Blessed are the peacemakers,
for they shall be called children of God.
Blessed are they who are persecuted for the sake of righteousness,
for theirs is the Kingdom of Heaven.

▷ *page 58*

PRAYER AFTER COMMUNION

Renewed by this bread from the heavenly table,
we beseech you, Lord,
that, being the food of charity,
it may confirm our hearts
and stir us to serve you in our neighbour.
Through Christ our Lord.   **Amen.**

▷ *page 59*

ORDINARY

TWENTY-THIRD SUNDAY IN ORDINARY TIME

ENTRANCE ANTIPHON   *Psalm 118:137, 124*

You are just, O Lord, and your judgement is right;
treat your servant in accord with your merciful love.

▷ *page 7*

COLLECT

O God, by whom we are redeemed and receive adoption,
look graciously upon your beloved sons and daughters,
that those who believe in Christ
may receive true freedom
and an everlasting inheritance.
Through our Lord Jesus Christ, your Son,
who lives and reigns with you in the unity of the Holy Spirit,
one God, for ever and ever.   **Amen.**

FIRST READING   *Ezekiel 33:7–9*

If you do not speak to the wicked man, I will hold you responsible for his death.

The word of the Lord was addressed to me as follows, 'Son of man, I have appointed you as sentry to the House of Israel. When you hear a word from my mouth, warn them in my name. If I say to a wicked man: Wicked wretch, you are to die, and you do not speak to warn the wicked man to renounce his ways, then he shall die for his sin, but I will hold you responsible for his death. If, however, you do warn a wicked man to renounce his ways and repent, and he does not repent, then he shall die for his sin, but you yourself will have saved your life.'

The word of the Lord.
Thanks be to God.

RESPONSORIAL PSALM   *Psalm 94:1–2, 6–9 response vv 7–8*

> **O that today you would listen to his voice!**
> **Harden not your hearts.**

1   Come, ring out our joy to the Lord;
    hail the rock who saves us.
    Let us come before him, giving thanks,
    with songs let us hail the Lord.

2   Come in; let us bow and bend low,
    let us kneel before the God who made us
    for he is our God and we
    the people who belong to his pasture,
    the flock that is led by his hand.

3   O that today you would listen to his voice!
    'Harden not your hearts as at Meribah,
    as on that day at Massah in the desert
    when your fathers put me to the test;
    when they tried me, though they saw my work.'

SECOND READING   *Romans 13:8–10*

Love is the answer to every one of the commandments.

Avoid getting into debt, except the debt of mutual love. If you love your fellow men you have carried out your obligations. All the commandments: You shall not commit adultery, you shall not kill, you shall not steal, you shall not covet, and so on, are summed up in this single command: You must love your neighbour as yourself. Love is the one thing that cannot hurt your neighbour; that is why it is the answer to every one of the commandments.

The word of the Lord.
Thanks be to God.

GOSPEL ACCLAMATION   *John 17:17*

> **Alleluia, alleluia!**
> **Your word is truth, O Lord,**
> **consecrate us in the truth.**
> **Alleluia!**

or   *2 Corinthians 5:19*

> **Alleluia, alleluia!**
> **God in Christ was reconciling the world to himself,**
> **and he has entrusted to us the news that they are reconciled.**
> **Alleluia!**

GOSPEL   *Matthew 18:15–20*

The Lord be with you.
And with your spirit.

A reading from the holy Gospel according to Matthew.
Glory to you, O Lord.

If he listens to you, you have won back your brother.

Jesus said to his disciples: 'If your brother does something wrong, go and have it out with him alone, between your two selves. If he listens to you, you have won back your brother. If he does not listen, take one or two others along with you: the evidence of two or three witnesses is required to sustain any charge. But if he refuses to listen to these, report it to the community; and if he refuses to listen to the community, treat him like a pagan or a tax collector.

'I tell you solemnly, whatever you bind on earth shall be considered bound in heaven; whatever you loose on earth shall be considered loosed in heaven.

'I tell you solemnly once again, if two of you on earth agree to ask anything at all, it will be granted to you by my Father in heaven. For where two or three meet in my name, I shall be there with them.'

The Gospel of the Lord.
Praise to you, Lord Jesus Christ.

▷ *page 11*

ORDINARY

PRAYER OVER THE OFFERINGS

O God, who give us the gift of true prayer and of peace,
graciously grant that through this offering,
we may do fitting homage to your divine majesty
and, by partaking of the sacred mystery,
we may be faithfully united in mind and heart.
Through Christ our Lord.   **Amen.**

▷ *page 15*

COMMUNION ANTIPHON   *cf Psalm 41:2–3*

Like the deer that yearns for running streams,
so my soul is yearning for you, my God;
my soul is thirsting for God, the living God.

or   John 8:12

I am the light of the world, says the Lord;
whoever follows me will not walk in darkness,
but will have the light of life.

▷ *page 58*

PRAYER AFTER COMMUNION

Grant that your faithful, O Lord,
whom you nourish and endow with life
through the food of your Word and heavenly Sacrament,
may so benefit from your beloved Son's great gifts
that we may merit an eternal share in his life.
Who lives and reigns for ever and ever. **Amen.**

▷ *page 59*

TWENTY-FOURTH SUNDAY IN ORDINARY TIME

ENTRANCE ANTIPHON *cf Sirach 36:18*

Give peace, O Lord, to those who wait for you,
that your prophets be found true.
Hear the prayers of your servant,
and of your people Israel.

▷ *page 7*

COLLECT

Look upon us, O God,
Creator and ruler of all things,
and, that we may feel the working of your mercy,
grant that we may serve you with all our heart.
Through our Lord Jesus Christ, your Son,
who lives and reigns with you in the unity of the Holy Spirit,
one God, for ever and ever. **Amen.**

FIRST READING *Ecclesiasticus 27:30–28:7*

Forgive your neighbour the hurt he does you, and when you pray, your sins will be forgiven.

Resentment and anger, these are foul things, and both are found with the sinner. He who exacts vengeance will experience the vengeance of the Lord, who keeps strict account of sin. Forgive your neighbour the hurt he does you, and when you pray, your sins will be forgiven. If a man nurses anger against another, can he then demand compassion from the Lord? Showing no pity for a man like himself, can he then plead for his own sins? Mere creature of flesh, he cherishes resentment; who will forgive him his sins? Remember the last things, and stop hating, remember dissolution and death, and live by the commandments. Remember the commandments, and do not bear your neighbour ill-will; remember the covenant of the Most High, and overlook the offence.

The word of the Lord.
Thanks be to God.

RESPONSORIAL PSALM   *Psalm 102:1–4, 9–12 response v 8*

> **The Lord is compassion and love,**
> **slow to anger and rich in mercy.**

1   My soul, give thanks to the Lord,
    all my being, bless his holy name.
    My soul, give thanks to the Lord
    and never forget all his blessings.

2   It is he who forgives all your guilt,
    who heals every one of your ills,
    who redeems your life from the grave,
    who crowns you with love and compassion.

3   His wrath will come to an end;
    he will not be angry for ever.
    He does not treat us according to our sins
    nor repay us according to our faults.

4   For as the heavens are high above the earth
    so strong is his love for those who fear him.
    As far as the east is from the west
    so far does he remove our sins.

SECOND READING   *Romans 14:7–9*

Alive or dead we belong to the Lord.

The life and death of each of us has its influence on others; if we live, we live for the Lord; and if we die, we die for the Lord, so that alive or dead we belong to the Lord. This explains why Christ both died and came to life, it was so that he might be Lord both of the dead and of the living.

The word of the Lord.
Thanks be to God.

GOSPEL ACCLAMATION   *I Samuel 3:9, John 6:68*

> **Alleluia, alleluia!**
> **Speak, Lord, your servant is listening;**
> **you have the message of eternal life.**
> **Alleluia!**

or   *John 13:34*

> **Alleluia, alleluia!**
> **I give you a new commandment:**
> **love one another, just as I have loved you,**
> **says the Lord.**
> **Alleluia!**

ORDINARY

GOSPEL *Matthew 18:21–35*

The Lord be with you.
And with your spirit.

A reading from the holy Gospel according to Matthew.
Glory to you, O Lord.

I do not tell you to forgive seven times, but seventy-seven times.

Peter went up to Jesus and said, 'Lord, how often must I forgive my brother if he wrongs me? As often as seven times?' Jesus answered, 'Not seven, I tell you, but seventy-seven times.

'And so the kingdom of heaven may be compared to a king who decided to settle his accounts with his servants. When the reckoning began, they brought him a man who owed ten thousand talents; but he had no means of paying, so his master gave orders that he should be sold, together with his wife and children and all his possessions, to meet the debt. At this, the servant threw himself down at his master's feet. "Give me time," he said, "and I will pay the whole sum." And the servant's master felt so sorry for him that he let him go and cancelled the debt. Now as this servant went out, he happened to meet a fellow servant who owed him one hundred denarii; and he seized him by the throat and began to throttle him. "Pay what you owe me," he said. His fellow servant fell at his feet and implored him, saying, "Give me time and I will pay you." But the other would not agree; on the contrary, he had him thrown into prison till he should pay the debt. His fellow servants were deeply distressed when they saw what had happened, and they went to their master and reported the whole affair to him. Then the master sent for him. "You wicked servant," he said, "I cancelled all that debt of yours when you appealed to me. Were you not bound, then, to have pity on your fellow servant just as I had pity on you?" And in his anger the master handed him over to the torturers till he should pay all his debt. And this is how my heavenly Father will deal with you unless you each forgive your brother from your heart.'

The Gospel of the Lord.
Praise to you, Lord Jesus Christ.

▷ *page 11*

PRAYER OVER THE OFFERINGS

Look with favour on our supplications, O Lord,
and in your kindness accept these, your servants' offerings,
that what each has offered to the honour of your name
may serve the salvation of all.
Through Christ our Lord. **Amen.**

▷ *page 15*

COMMUNION ANTIPHON   *cf Psalm 35:8*

How precious is your mercy, O God!
The children of men seek shelter in the shadow of your wings.

or   cf 1 Corinthians 10:16

The chalice of blessing that we bless
is a communion in the Blood of Christ;
and the bread that we break
is a sharing in the Body of the Lord.

▷ *page 58*

PRAYER AFTER COMMUNION

May the working of this heavenly gift, O Lord, we pray,
take possession of our minds and bodies,
so that its effects, and not our own desires,
may always prevail in us.
Through Christ our Lord.   **Amen.**

▷ *page 59*

TWENTY-FIFTH SUNDAY IN ORDINARY TIME

ENTRANCE ANTIPHON

I am the salvation of the people, says the Lord.
Should they cry to me in any distress,
I will hear them, and I will be their Lord for ever.

▷ *page 7*

COLLECT

O God, who founded all the commands of your sacred Law
upon love of you and of our neighbour,
grant that, by keeping your precepts,
we may merit to attain eternal life.
Through our Lord Jesus Christ, your Son,
who lives and reigns with you in the unity of the Holy Spirit,
one God, for ever and ever.   **Amen.**

FIRST READING   *Isaiah 55:6–9*

My thoughts are not your thoughts.

Seek the Lord while he is still to be found, call to him while he is still near. Let the wicked man abandon his way, the evil man his thoughts. Let him turn back to the Lord who will take pity on him, to our God who is rich in forgiving; for my thoughts are not your thoughts, my ways not your ways – it is the Lord who speaks. Yes, the heavens are as high above earth as my ways are above your ways, my thoughts above your thoughts.

The word of the Lord.
Thanks be to God.

RESPONSORIAL PSALM   *Psalm 144:2–3, 8–9, 17–18 response v 18*

The Lord is close to all who call him.

1   I will bless you day after day
    and praise your name for ever.
    The Lord is great, highly to be praised,
    his greatness cannot be measured.

2   The Lord is kind and full of compassion,
    slow to anger, abounding in love.
    How good is the Lord to all,
    compassionate to all his creatures.

3   The Lord is just in all his ways
    and loving in all his deeds.
    He is close to all who call him,
    who call on him from their hearts.

SECOND READING   *Philippians 1:20–24, 27*

Life to me is Christ.

Christ will be glorified in my body, whether by my life or by my death. Life to me, of course, is Christ, but then death would bring me something more; but then again, if living in this body means doing work which is having good results – I do not know what I should choose. I am caught in this dilemma: I want to be gone and be with Christ, which would be very much better, but for me to stay alive in this body is a more urgent need for your sake.

Avoid anything in your everyday lives that would be unworthy of the gospel of Christ.

The word of the Lord.
Thanks be to God.

GOSPEL ACCLAMATION   *Luke 19:38*

Alleluia, alleluia!
Blessings on the King who comes,
in the name of the Lord!
Peace in heaven
and glory in the highest heavens!
Alleluia!

or   *cf Acts 16:14*

Alleluia, alleluia!
Open our heart, O Lord,
to accept the words of your Son.
Alleluia!

GOSPEL　*Matthew 20:1–16*

The Lord be with you.
And with your spirit.

A reading from the holy Gospel according to Matthew.
Glory to you, O Lord.

Why be envious because I am generous?

Jesus said to his disciples: 'The kingdom of heaven is like a landowner going out at daybreak to hire workers for his vineyard. He made an agreement with the workers for one denarius a day, and sent them to his vineyard. Going out at about the third hour he saw others standing idle in the market place and said to them, "You go to my vineyard too and I will give you a fair wage." So they went. At about the sixth hour and again at about the ninth hour, he went out and did the same. Then at about the eleventh hour he went out and found more men standing round, and he said to them, "Why have you been standing here idle all day?" "Because no one has hired us," they answered. He said to them, "You go into my vineyard too." In the evening, the owner of the vineyard said to his bailiff, "Call the workers and pay them their wages, starting with the last arrivals and ending with the first." So those who were hired at about the eleventh hour came forward and received one denarius each. When the first came, they expected to get more, but they too received one denarius each. They took it, but grumbled at the landowner. "The men who came last" they said "have done only one hour, and you have treated them the same as us, though we have done a heavy day's work in all the heat." He answered one of them and said, "My friend, I am not being unjust to you; did we not agree on one denarius? Take your earnings and go. I choose to pay the last-comer as much as I pay you. Have I no right to do what I like with my own? Why be envious because I am generous?" Thus the last will be first, and the first, last.'

The Gospel of the Lord.
Praise to you, Lord Jesus Christ.

▷ *page 11*

PRAYER OVER THE OFFERINGS

Receive with favour, O Lord, we pray,
the offerings of your people,
that what they profess with devotion and faith
may be theirs through these heavenly mysteries.
Through Christ our Lord.　**Amen.**

▷ *page 15*

COMMUNION ANTIPHON　*Psalm 118:4–5*

You have laid down your precepts to be carefully kept;
may my ways be firm in keeping your statutes.

or　*John 10:14*

I am the Good Shepherd, says the Lord;
I know my sheep, and mine know me.

▷ *page 58*

ORDINARY

PRAYER AFTER COMMUNION
Graciously raise up, O Lord,
those you renew with this Sacrament,
that we may come to possess your redemption
both in mystery and in the manner of our life.
Through Christ our Lord. **Amen.**

▷ *page 59*

TWENTY-SIXTH SUNDAY IN ORDINARY TIME

ENTRANCE ANTIPHON   *Daniel 3:31, 29, 30, 43, 42*
All that you have done to us, O Lord,
you have done with true judgement,
for we have sinned against you
and not obeyed your commandments.
But give glory to your name
and deal with us according to the bounty of your mercy.

▷ *page 7*

COLLECT
O God, who manifest your almighty power
above all by pardoning and showing mercy,
bestow, we pray, your grace abundantly upon us
and make those hastening to attain your promises
heirs to the treasures of heaven.
Through our Lord Jesus Christ, your Son,
who lives and reigns with you in the unity of the Holy Spirit,
one God, for ever and ever. **Amen.**

FIRST READING   *Ezekiel 18:25–28*
When the sinner renounces sin, he shall certainly live.

The word of the Lord was addressed to me as follows: 'You object, "What the Lord does is unjust." Listen, you House of Israel: is what I do unjust? Is it not what you do that is unjust? When the upright man renounces his integrity to commit sin and dies because of this, he dies because of the evil that he himself has committed. When the sinner renounces sin to become law-abiding and honest, he deserves to live. He has chosen to renounce all his previous sins; he shall certainly live; he shall not die.'

The word of the Lord.
Thanks be to God.

RESPONSORIAL PSALM   *Psalm 24:4–9 response v 6*

Remember your mercy, Lord.

1   Lord, make me know your ways.
    Lord, teach me your paths.
    Make me walk in your truth, and teach me:
    for you are God my saviour.

2   Remember your mercy, Lord,
    and the love you have shown from of old.
    Do not remember the sins of my youth.
    In your love remember me,
    because of your goodness, O Lord.

3   The Lord is good and upright.
    He shows the path to those who stray,
    he guides the humble in the right path;
    he teaches his way to the poor.

SECOND READING   *Philippians 2:1–11   Shorter form (omitting oblique text): Philippians 2:1–5*

In your minds you must be the same as Christ Jesus.

If our life in Christ means anything to you, if love can persuade at all, or the Spirit that we have in common, or any tenderness and sympathy, then be united in your convictions and united in your love, with a common purpose and a common mind. That is the one thing which would make me completely happy. There must be no competition among you, no conceit; but everybody is to be self-effacing. Always consider the other person to be better than yourself, so that nobody thinks of his own interests first but everybody thinks of other people's interests instead. In your minds you must be the same as Christ Jesus.

His state was divine, yet he did not cling to his equality with God but emptied himself to assume the condition of a slave, and became as men are; and being as all men are, he was humbler yet, even to accepting death, death on a cross. But God raised him high and gave him the name which is above all other names so that all beings in the heavens, on earth and in the underworld, should bend the knee at the name of Jesus and that every tongue should acclaim Jesus Christ as Lord, to the glory of God the Father.

The word of the Lord.
Thanks be to God.

GOSPEL ACCLAMATION   *John 14:23*

Alleluia, alleluia!
If anyone loves me he will keep my word,
and my Father will love him,
and we shall come to him.
Alleluia!

or   *John 10:27*

Alleluia, alleluia!
The sheep that belong to me listen to my voice,
says the Lord.
I know them and they follow me.
Alleluia!

GOSPEL   *Matthew 21:28–32*

The Lord be with you.
And with your spirit.

A reading from the holy Gospel according to Matthew.
Glory to you, O Lord.

He thought better of it and went.
Tax collectors and prostitutes are making their way into the kingdom of God before you.

Jesus said to the chief priests and the elders of the people, 'What is your opinion? A man had two sons. He went and said to the first, "My boy, you go and work in the vineyard today." He answered, "I will not go", but afterwards thought better of it and went. The man then went and said the same thing to the second who answered, "Certainly sir", but did not go. Which of the two did the father's will?' 'The first,' they said. Jesus said to them, 'I tell you solemnly, tax collectors and prostitutes are making their way into the kingdom of God before you. For John came to you, a pattern of true righteousness, but you did not believe him, and yet the tax collectors and prostitutes did. Even after seeing that, you refused to think better of it and believe in him.'

The Gospel of the Lord.
Praise to you, Lord Jesus Christ.

▷ *page 11*

PRAYER OVER THE OFFERINGS

Grant us, O merciful God,
that this our offering may find acceptance with you
and that through it the wellspring of all blessing
may be laid open before us.
Through Christ our Lord. **Amen.**

▷ *page 15*

COMMUNION ANTIPHON   *cf Psalm 118:49–50*

Remember your word to your servant, O Lord,
by which you have given me hope.
This is my comfort when I am brought low.

or   *1 John 3:16*

By this we came to know the love of God:
that Christ laid down his life for us;
so we ought to lay down our lives for one another.

▷ *page 58*

PRAYER AFTER COMMUNION

May this heavenly mystery, O Lord,
restore us in mind and body,
that we may be coheirs in glory with Christ,
to whose suffering we are united
whenever we proclaim his Death.
Who lives and reigns for ever and ever. **Amen.**

▷ *page 59*

TWENTY-SEVENTH SUNDAY IN ORDINARY TIME

ENTRANCE ANTIPHON *cf Esther 4:17*

Within your will, O Lord, all things are established,
and there is none that can resist your will.
For you have made all things, the heaven and the earth,
and all that is held within the circle of heaven;
you are the Lord of all.

▷ *page 7*

COLLECT

Almighty ever-living God,
who in the abundance of your kindness
surpass the merits and the desires of those who entreat you,
pour out your mercy upon us
to pardon what conscience dreads
and to give what prayer does not dare to ask.
Through our Lord Jesus Christ, your Son,
who lives and reigns with you in the unity of the Holy Spirit,
one God, for ever and ever. **Amen.**

FIRST READING *Isaiah 5:1–7*

The vineyard of the Lord of hosts is the House of Israel.

Let me sing to my friend the song of his love for his vineyard. My friend had a vineyard on a fertile hillside. He dug the soil, cleared it of stones, and planted choice vines in it. In the middle he built a tower, he dug a press there too. He expected it to yield grapes, but sour grapes were all that it gave.

And now, inhabitants of Jerusalem and men of Judah, I ask you to judge between my vineyard and me. What could I have done for my vineyard that I have not done? I expected it to yield grapes. Why did it yield sour grapes instead?

Very well, I will tell you what I am going to do to my vineyard: I will take away its hedge for it to be grazed on, and knock down its wall for it to be trampled on. I will lay it waste, unpruned, undug; overgrown by the briar and the thorn. I will command the clouds to rain no rain on it. Yes, the vineyard of the Lord of hosts is the House of Israel, and the men of Judah that chosen plant. He expected justice, but found bloodshed, integrity, but only a cry of distress.

The word of the Lord.
Thanks be to God.

RESPONSORIAL PSALM *Psalm 79:9, 12–16, 19–20 response Isaiah 5:7*

The vineyard of the Lord is the House of Israel.

1 You brought a vine out of Egypt,
   to plant it you drove out the nations.
   It stretched out its branches to the sea,
   to the Great River it stretched out its shoots.

continued…

ORDINARY

The vineyard of the Lord is the House of Israel.

2   Then why have you broken down its walls?
     It is plucked by all who pass by.
     It is ravaged by the boar of the forest,
     devoured by the beasts of the field.

2   God of hosts, turn again, we implore,
     look down from heaven and see.
     Visit this vine and protect it,
     the vine your right hand has planted.

4   And we shall never forsake you again:
     give us life that we may call upon your name.
     God of hosts, bring us back;
     let your face shine on us and we shall be saved.

SECOND READING   *Philippians 4:6–9*

The God of peace will be with you.

There is no need to worry; but if there is anything you need, pray for it, asking God for it with prayer and thanksgiving, and that peace of God, which is so much greater than we can understand, will guard your hearts and your thoughts, in Christ Jesus. Finally, brothers, fill your minds with everything that is true, everything that is noble, everything that is good and pure, everything that we love and honour, and everything that can be thought virtuous or worthy of praise. Keep doing all the things that you learnt from me and have been taught by me and have heard or seen that I do. Then the God of peace will be with you.

The word of the Lord.
Thanks be to God.

GOSPEL ACCLAMATION   *John 15:15*

**Alleluia, alleluia!
I call you friends, says the Lord,
because I have made known to you
everything I have learnt from my Father.
Alleluia!**

or   *cf John 15:16*

**Alleluia, alleluia!
I chose you from the world
to go out and bear fruit,
fruit that will last,
says the Lord.
Alleluia!**

GOSPEL   *Matthew 21:33–43*

The Lord be with you.
And with your spirit.

A reading from the holy Gospel according to Matthew.
Glory to you, O Lord.

He will lease the vineyard to other tenants.

Jesus said to the chief priests and the elders of the people, 'Listen to another parable. There was a man, a landowner, who planted a vineyard; he fenced it round, dug a winepress in it and built a tower; then he leased it to tenants and went abroad. When vintage time drew near he sent his servants to the tenants to collect his produce. But the tenants seized his servants, thrashed one, killed another and stoned a third. Next he sent some more servants, this time a larger number, and they dealt with them in the same way. Finally he sent his son to them. "They will respect my son" he said. But when the tenants saw the son, they said to each other, "This is the heir. Come on, let us kill him and take over his inheritance." So they seized him and threw him out of the vineyard and killed him. Now when the owner of the vineyard comes, what will he do to those tenants?' They answered, 'He will bring those wretches to a wretched end and lease the vineyard to other tenants who will deliver the produce to him when the season arrives.' Jesus said to them, 'Have you never read in the scriptures:

It was the stone rejected by the builders that became the keystone. This was the Lord's doing and it is wonderful to see?

'I tell you, then, that the kingdom of God will be taken from you and given to a people who will produce its fruit.'

The Gospel of the Lord.
Praise to you, Lord Jesus Christ.

▷ *page 11*

PRAYER OVER THE OFFERINGS

Accept, O Lord, we pray,
the sacrifices instituted by your commands
and, through the sacred mysteries,
which we celebrate with dutiful service,
graciously complete the sanctifying work
by which you are pleased to redeem us.
Through Christ our Lord.   **Amen.**

▷ *page 15*

COMMUNION ANTIPHON   *Lamentations 3:25*

The Lord is good to those who hope in him,
to the soul that seeks him.

or   *cf 1 Corinthians 10:17*

Though many, we are one bread, one body,
for we all partake of the one Bread and one Chalice.

▷ *page 58*

PRAYER AFTER COMMUNION

Grant us, almighty God,
that we may be refreshed and nourished
by the Sacrament which we have received,
so as to be transformed into what we consume.
Through Christ our Lord. **Amen.**

▷ *page 59*

TWENTY-EIGHTH SUNDAY IN ORDINARY TIME

ENTRANCE ANTIPHON   *Psalm 129:3–4*

If you, O Lord, should mark iniquities,
Lord, who could stand?
But with you is found forgiveness,
O God of Israel.

▷ *page 7*

COLLECT

May your grace, O Lord, we pray,
at all times go before us and follow after
and make us always determined
to carry out good works.
Through our Lord Jesus Christ, your Son,
who lives and reigns with you in the unity of the Holy Spirit,
one God, for ever and ever. **Amen.**

FIRST READING   *Isaiah 25:6–10*

The Lord will prepare a banquet, and will wipe away tears from every cheek.

On this mountain, the Lord of hosts will prepare for all people a banquet of rich food, a banquet of fine wines, of food rich and juicy, of fine strained wines. On this mountain he will remove the mourning veil covering all peoples, and the shroud enwrapping all nations, he will destroy Death for ever. The Lord will wipe away the tears from every cheek; he will take away his people's shame everywhere on earth, for the Lord has said so. That day, it will be said: See, this is our God in whom we hoped for salvation; the Lord is the one in whom we hoped. We exult and we rejoice that he has saved us; for the hand of the Lord rests on this mountain.

The word of the Lord.
Thanks be to God.

RESPONSORIAL PSALM   *Psalm 22 response v 6*

**In the Lord's own house shall I dwell
for ever and ever.**

1   The Lord is my shepherd;
    there is nothing I shall want.
    Fresh and green are the pastures
    where he gives me repose.
    Near restful waters he leads me,
    to revive my drooping spirit.

2   He guides me along the right path;
    he is true to his name.
    If I should walk in the valley of darkness
    no evil would I fear.
    You are there with your crook and your staff;
    with these you give me comfort.

3   You have prepared a banquet for me
    in the sight of my foes.
    My head you have anointed with oil;
    my cup is overflowing.

4   Surely goodness and kindness shall follow me
    all the days of my life.
    In the Lord's own house shall I dwell
    for ever and ever.

SECOND READING   *Philippians 4:12–14, 19–20*

There is nothing I cannot master with the help of the One who gives me strength.

I know how to be poor and I know how to be rich too. I have been through my initiation and now I am ready for anything anywhere: full stomach or empty stomach, poverty or plenty. There is nothing I cannot master with the help of the One who gives me strength. All the same, it was good of you to share with me in my hardships. In return my God will fulfil all your needs, in Christ Jesus, as lavishly as only God can. Glory to God, our Father, for ever and ever. Amen.

The word of the Lord.
Thanks be to God.

GOSPEL ACCLAMATION *John 1:14, 12*

Alleluia, alleluia!
The Word was made flesh and lived among us;
to all who did accept him
he gave power to become children of God.
Alleluia!

or *Ephesians 1:17, 18*

Alleluia, alleluia!
May the Father of our Lord Jesus Christ
enlighten the eyes of our mind,
so that we can see what hope his call holds for us.
Alleluia!

GOSPEL *Matthew 22:1–14 Shorter form (omitting oblique text): Matthew 22:1–10*

The Lord be with you.
And with your spirit.

A reading from the holy Gospel according to Matthew.
Glory to you, O Lord.

Invite everyone you can find to the wedding.

Jesus said to the chief priests and elders of the people: 'The kingdom of heaven may be compared to a king who gave a feast for his son's wedding. He sent his servants to call those who had been invited, but they would not come. Next he sent some more servants. "Tell those who have been invited" he said "that I have my banquet all prepared, my oxen and fattened cattle have been slaughtered, everything is ready. Come to the wedding." But they were not interested: one went off to his farm, another to his business, and the rest seized his servants, maltreated them and killed them. The king was furious. He despatched his troops, destroyed those murderers and burnt their town. Then he said to his servants, "The wedding is ready; but as those who were invited proved to be unworthy, go to the crossroads in the town and invite everyone you can find to the wedding." So these servants went out on to the roads and collected together everyone they could find, bad and good alike; and the wedding hall was filled with guests. *When the king came in to look at the guests he noticed one man who was not wearing a wedding garment, and said to him, "How did you get in here, my friend, without a wedding garment?" And the man was silent. Then the king said to the attendants, "Bind him hand and foot and throw him out into the dark, where there will be weeping and grinding of teeth." For many are called, but few are chosen.'*

The Gospel of the Lord.
Praise to you, Lord Jesus Christ.

▷ *page 11*

PRAYER OVER THE OFFERINGS

Accept, O Lord, the prayers of your faithful
with the sacrificial offerings,
that, through these acts of devotedness,
we may pass over to the glory of heaven.
Through Christ our Lord. **Amen.**

▷ *page 15*

COMMUNION ANTIPHON   *cf Psalm 33:11*

The rich suffer want and go hungry,
but those who seek the Lord lack no blessing.

or   *1 John 3:2*

When the Lord appears, we shall be like him,
for we shall see him as he is.

▷ *page 58*

PRAYER AFTER COMMUNION

We entreat your majesty most humbly, O Lord,
that, as you feed us with the nourishment
which comes from the most holy Body and Blood of your Son,
so you may make us sharers of his divine nature.
Who lives and reigns for ever and ever. **Amen.**

▷ *page 59*

ORDINARY

TWENTY-NINTH SUNDAY IN ORDINARY TIME

ENTRANCE ANTIPHON   *cf Psalm 16:6, 8*

To you I call; for you will surely heed me, O God;
turn your ear to me; hear my words.
Guard me as the apple of your eye;
in the shadow of your wings protect me.

▷ *page 7*

COLLECT

Almighty ever-living God,
grant that we may always conform our will to yours
and serve your majesty in sincerity of heart.
Through our Lord Jesus Christ, your Son,
who lives and reigns with you in the unity of the Holy Spirit,
one God, for ever and ever. **Amen.**

FIRST READING   *Isaiah 45:1, 4–6*

I have taken Cyrus by his right hand to subdue nations before him.

Thus says the Lord to his anointed, to Cyrus, whom he has taken by his right hand to subdue nations before him and strip the loins of kings, to force gateways before him that their gates be closed no more:

It is for the sake of my servant Jacob, of Israel my chosen one, that I have called you by your name, conferring a title though you do not know me. I am the Lord, unrivalled; there is no other God besides me. Though you do not know me, I arm you that men may know from the rising to the setting of the sun that, apart from me, all is nothing.

The word of the Lord.
Thanks be to God.

RESPONSORIAL PSALM   *Psalm 95: 1, 3–5, 7–10 response v 7*

Give the Lord glory and power.

1   O sing a new song to the Lord,
   sing to the Lord all the earth.
   Tell among the nations his glory
   and his wonders among all the peoples.

2   The Lord is great and worthy of praise,
   to be feared above all gods;
   the gods of the heathens are naught.
   It was the Lord who made the heavens.

3   Give the Lord, you families of peoples,
   give the Lord glory and power,
   give the Lord the glory of his name.
   Bring an offering and enter his courts.

4   Worship the Lord in his temple.
   O earth, tremble before him.
   Proclaim to the nations: 'God is king.'
   He will judge the peoples in fairness.

SECOND READING   *1 Thessalonians 1:1–5*

We constantly remember your faith, your love and your hope.

From Paul, Silvanus and Timothy, to the Church in Thessalonika which is in God the Father and the Lord Jesus Christ; wishing you grace and peace from God the Father and the Lord Jesus Christ.

We always mention you in our prayers and thank God for you all, and constantly remember before God our Father how you have shown your faith in action, worked for love and persevered through hope, in our Lord Jesus Christ.

We know, brothers, that God loves you and that you have been chosen, because when we brought the Good News to you, it came to you not only as words, but as power and as the Holy Spirit and as utter conviction.

The word of the Lord.
Thanks be to God.

GOSPEL ACCLAMATION   *John 17:17*

Alleluia, alleluia!
Your word is truth, O Lord,
consecrate us in the truth.
Alleluia!

or   *Philippians 2:15–16*

Alleluia, alleluia!
You will shine in the world like bright stars
because you are offering it the word of life.
Alleluia!

GOSPEL   *Matthew 22:15–21*

The Lord be with you.
And with your spirit.

A reading from the holy Gospel according to Matthew.
Glory to you, O Lord.

Give back to Caesar what belongs to Caesar – and to God what belongs to God.

The Pharisees went away to work out between them how to trap Jesus in what he said. And they sent their disciples to him, together with the Herodians, to say, 'Master, we know that you are an honest man and teach the way of God in an honest way, and that you are not afraid of anyone, because a man's rank means nothing to you. Tell us your opinion, then. Is it permissible to pay taxes to Caesar or not?' But Jesus was aware of their malice and replied, 'You hypocrites! Why do you set this trap for me? Let me see the money you pay the tax with.' They handed him a denarius, and he said, 'Whose head is this? Whose name?' 'Caesar's,' they replied. He then said to them, 'Very well, give back to Caesar what belongs to Caesar – and to God what belongs to God.'

The Gospel of the Lord.
Praise to you, Lord Jesus Christ.

▷ *page 11*

PRAYER OVER THE OFFERINGS

Grant us, Lord, we pray,
a sincere respect for your gifts,
that, through the purifying action of your grace,
we may be cleansed by the very mysteries we serve.
Through Christ our Lord. **Amen.**

▷ *page 15*

COMMUNION ANTIPHON   *cf Psalm 32:18–19*

Behold, the eyes of the Lord
are on those who fear him,
who hope in his merciful love,
to rescue their souls from death,
to keep them alive in famine.

or   *Mark 10:45*

The Son of Man has come
to give his life as a ransom for many.

▷ *page 58*

PRAYER AFTER COMMUNION

Grant, O Lord, we pray,
that, benefiting from participation in heavenly things,
we may be helped by what you give in this present age
and prepared for the gifts that are eternal.
Through Christ our Lord.   **Amen.**

▷ *page 59*

 THIRTIETH SUNDAY IN ORDINARY TIME

ENTRANCE ANTIPHON   *cf Psalm 104:3–4*

Let the hearts that seek the Lord rejoice;
turn to the Lord and his strength;
constantly seek his face.

▷ *page 7*

COLLECT

Almighty ever-living God,
increase our faith, hope and charity,
and make us love what you command,
so that we may merit what you promise.
Through our Lord Jesus Christ, your Son,
who lives and reigns with you in the unity of the Holy Spirit,
one God, for ever and ever.   **Amen.**

FIRST READING   *Exodus 22:20–26*

If you are harsh with the widow, the orphan, my anger will flare against you.

The Lord said to Moses, 'Tell the sons of Israel this, "You must not molest the stranger or oppress him, for you lived as strangers in the land of Egypt. You must not be harsh with the widow, or with the orphan; if you are harsh with them, they will surely cry out to me, and be sure I shall hear their cry; my anger will flare and I shall kill you with the sword, your own wives will be widows, your own children orphans.

"If you lend money to any of my people, to any poor man among you, you must not play the usurer with him: you must not demand interest from him.

"If you take another's cloak as a pledge, you must give it back to him before sunset. It is all the covering he has; it is the cloak he wraps his body in; what else would he sleep in? If he cries to me, I will listen, for I am full of pity." '

The word of the Lord.
Thanks be to God.

RESPONSORIAL PSALM   *Psalm 17:2–4, 47, 51 response v 2*

I love you, Lord, my strength.

1   I love you, Lord, my strength,
   my rock, my fortress, my saviour.
   My God is the rock where I take refuge;
   my shield, my mighty help, my stronghold.
   The Lord is worthy of all praise:
   when I call I am saved from my foes.

2   Long life to the Lord, my rock!
   Praised be the God who saves me.
   He has given great victories to his king
   and shown his love for his anointed.

SECOND READING   *1 Thessalonians 1:5–10*
You broke with idolatry and became servants of God; you are now waiting for his Son.

You observed the sort of life we lived when we were with you, which was for your instruction, and you were led to become imitators of us, and of the Lord; and it was with the joy of the Holy Spirit that you took to the gospel, in spite of the great opposition all round you. This has made you the great example to all believers in Macedonia and Achaia since it was from you that the word of the Lord started to spread – and not only throughout Macedonia and Achaia, for the news of your faith in God has spread everywhere. We do not need to tell other people about it: other people tell us how we started the work among you, how you broke with idolatry when you were converted to God and became servants of the real, living God; and how you are now waiting for Jesus, his Son, whom he raised from the dead, to come from heaven to save us from the retribution which is coming.

The word of the Lord.
Thanks be to God.

ORDINARY

GOSPEL ACCLAMATION   cf Acts 16:14

Alleluia, alleluia!
Open our heart, O Lord,
to accept the words of your Son.
Alleluia!

or   John 14:23

Alleluia, alleluia!
If anyone loves me he will keep my word,
and my Father will love him,
and we shall come to him.
Alleluia!

GOSPEL   Matthew 22:34–40

The Lord be with you.
And with your spirit.

A reading from the holy Gospel according to Matthew.
Glory to you, O Lord.

You must love the Lord your God and your neighbour as yourself.

When the Pharisees heard that Jesus had silenced the Sadducees they got together and, to disconcert him, one of them put a question, 'Master, which is the greatest commandment of the Law?' Jesus said, 'You must love the Lord your God with all your heart, with all your soul, and with all your mind. This is the greatest and the first commandment. The second resembles it: you must love your neighbour as yourself. On these two commandments hang the whole Law, and the Prophets also.'

The Gospel of the Lord.
Praise to you, Lord Jesus Christ.

▷ page 11

PRAYER OVER THE OFFERINGS

Look, we pray, O Lord,
on the offerings we make to your majesty,
that whatever is done by us in your service
may be directed above all to your glory.
Through Christ our Lord.   **Amen.**

▷ page 15

COMMUNION ANTIPHON   cf Psalm 19:6

We will ring out our joy at your saving help
and exult in the name of our God.

or   Ephesians 5:2

Christ loved us and gave himself up for us,
as a fragrant offering to God.

▷ page 58

PRAYER AFTER COMMUNION

May your Sacraments, O Lord, we pray,
perfect in us what lies within them,
that what we now celebrate in signs
we may one day possess in truth.
Through Christ our Lord. **Amen.**

▷ page 59

THIRTY-FIRST SUNDAY IN ORDINARY TIME

ORDINARY

ENTRANCE ANTIPHON   *cf Psalm 37:22–23*

Forsake me not, O Lord, my God;
be not far from me!
Make haste and come to my help,
O Lord, my strong salvation!

▷ page 7

COLLECT

Almighty and merciful God,
by whose gift your faithful offer you
right and praiseworthy service,
grant, we pray,
that we may hasten without stumbling
to receive the things you have promised.
Through our Lord Jesus Christ, your Son,
who lives and reigns with you in the unity of the Holy Spirit,
one God, for ever and ever. **Amen.**

FIRST READING   *Malachi 1:14–2:2, 8–10*

You have strayed from the way, you have caused many to stumble by your teaching.

I am a great king, says the Lord of hosts, and my name is feared throughout the nations. And now, priests, this warning is for you. If you do not listen, if you do not find it in your heart to glorify my name, says the Lord of hosts, I will send the curse on you and curse your very blessing. You have strayed from the way; you have caused many to stumble by your teaching. You have destroyed the covenant of Levi, says the Lord of hosts. And so I in my turn have made you contemptible and vile in the eyes of the whole people in repayment for the way you have not kept to my paths but have shown partiality in your administration.

Have we not all one Father? Did not one God create us? Why, then, do we break faith with one another, profaning the covenant of our ancestors?

The word of the Lord.
Thanks be to God.

RESPONSORIAL PSALM   *Psalm 130*

Keep my soul in peace before you, O Lord.

1   O Lord, my heart is not proud
nor haughty my eyes.
I have not gone after things too great
nor marvels beyond me.

2   Truly I have set my soul
in silence and peace.
A weaned child on its mother's breast,
even so is my soul.

3   O Israel, hope in the Lord
both now and for ever.

SECOND READING   *1 Thessalonians 2:7–9, 13*

We were eager to hand over to you not only the Good News but our whole lives as well.

Like a mother feeding and looking after her own children, we felt so devoted and protective towards you, and had come to love you so much, that we were eager to hand over to you not only the Good News but our whole lives as well. Let me remind you, brothers, how hard we used to work, slaving night and day so as not to be a burden on any one of you while we were proclaiming God's Good News to you.

Another reason why we constantly thank God for you is that as soon as you heard the message that we brought you as God's message, you accepted it for what it really is, God's message and not some human thinking; and it is still a living power among you who believe it.

The word of the Lord.
Thanks be to God.

GOSPEL ACCLAMATION   *I Samuel 3:9, John 6:68*

Alleluia, alleluia!
**Speak, Lord, your servant is listening;
you have the message of eternal life.**
Alleluia!

or   Matthew 23:9, 10

Alleluia, alleluia!
**You have only one Father, and he is in heaven;
you have only one Teacher, the Christ!**
Alleluia!

GOSPEL   *Matthew 23:1–12*

The Lord be with you.
And with your spirit.

A reading from the holy Gospel according to Matthew.
Glory to you, O Lord.

They do not practise what they preach.

Addressing the people and his disciples Jesus said, 'The scribes and the Pharisees occupy the chair of Moses. You must therefore do what they tell you and listen to what they say; but do not be guided by what they do: since they do not practise what they preach. They tie up heavy burdens and lay them on men's shoulders, but will they lift a finger to move them? Not they! Everything they do is done to attract attention, like wearing broader phylacteries and longer tassels, like wanting to take the place of honour at banquets and the front seats in the synagogues, being greeted obsequiously in the market squares and having people call them Rabbi.

'You, however, must not allow yourselves to be called Rabbi, since you have only one Master, and you are all brothers. You must call no one on earth your father, since you have only one Father, and he is in heaven. Nor must you allow yourselves to be called teachers, for you have only one Teacher, the Christ. The greatest among you must be your servant. Anyone who exalts himself will be humbled, and anyone who humbles himself will be exalted.'

The Gospel of the Lord.
Praise to you, Lord Jesus Christ.

▷ *page 11*

ORDINARY

PRAYER OVER THE OFFERINGS

May these sacrificial offerings, O Lord,
become for you a pure oblation,
and for us a holy outpouring of your mercy.
Through Christ our Lord.   **Amen.**

▷ *page 15*

COMMUNION ANTIPHON   *cf Psalm 15:11*

You will show me the path of life,
the fullness of joy in your presence, O Lord.

or   *John 6:58*

Just as the living Father sent me
and I have life because of the Father,
so whoever feeds on me
shall have life because of me, says the Lord.

▷ *page 58*

PRAYER AFTER COMMUNION

May the working of your power, O Lord,
increase in us, we pray,
so that, renewed by these heavenly Sacraments,
we may be prepared by your gift
for receiving what they promise.
Through Christ our Lord. **Amen.**

▷ *page 59*

THIRTY-SECOND SUNDAY IN ORDINARY TIME

ENTRANCE ANTIPHON   *cf Psalm 87:3*

Let my prayer come into your presence.
Incline your ear to my cry for help, O Lord.

▷ *page 7*

COLLECT

Almighty and merciful God,
graciously keep from us all adversity,
so that, unhindered in mind and body alike,
we may pursue in freedom of heart
the things that are yours.
Through our Lord Jesus Christ, your Son,
who lives and reigns with you in the unity of the Holy Spirit,
one God, for ever and ever. **Amen.**

FIRST READING   *Wisdom 6:12–16*

Wisdom is found by those who look for her.

Wisdom is bright, and does not grow dim. By those who love her she is readily seen, and found by those who look for her. Quick to anticipate those who desire her, she makes herself known to them. Watch for her early and you will have no trouble; you will find her sitting at your gates. Even to think about her is understanding fully grown; be on the alert for her and anxiety will quickly leave you. She herself walks about looking for those who are worthy of her and graciously shows herself to them as they go, in every thought of theirs coming to meet them.

The word of the Lord.
Thanks be to God.

RESPONSORIAL PSALM   *Psalm 62:2–8 response v 2*

For you my soul is thirsting, O God, my God.

1 O God, you are my God, for you I long;
   for you my soul is thirsting.
   My body pines for you
   like a dry, weary land without water.

2   So I gaze on you in the sanctuary
    to see your strength and your glory.
    For your love is better than life,
    my lips will speak your praise.

3   So I will bless you all my life,
    in your name I will lift up my hands.
    My soul shall be filled as with a banquet,
    my mouth shall praise you with joy.

4   On my bed I remember you.
    On you I muse through the night
    for you have been my help;
    in the shadow of your wings I rejoice.

ORDINARY

SECOND READING   *1 Thessalonians 4:13–18   Shorter form (omitting oblique text): 1 Thessalonians 4:13–14*
God will bring with him those who have died in Jesus.

We want you to be quite certain, brothers, about those who have died, to make sure that you do not grieve about them, like the other people who have no hope. We believe that Jesus died and rose again, and that it will be the same for those who have died in Jesus: God will bring them with him. *We can tell you this from the Lord's own teaching, that any of us who are left alive until the Lord's coming will not have any advantage over those who have died.* At the trumpet of God, the voice of the archangel will call out the command and the Lord himself will come down from heaven; those who have died in Christ will be the first to rise, and then those of us who are still alive will be taken up in the clouds, together with them, to meet the Lord in the air. So we shall stay with the Lord for ever. With such thoughts as these you should comfort one another.

The word of the Lord.
Thanks be to God.

GOSPEL ACCLAMATION   *Matthew 24:42, 44*

Alleluia, alleluia!
Stay awake and stand ready,
because you do not know the hour
when the Son of Man is coming.
Alleluia!

GOSPEL   *Matthew 25:1–13*
The Lord be with you.
And with your spirit.

A reading from the holy Gospel according to Matthew.
Glory to you, O Lord.
The bridegroom is here! Go out and meet him.

Jesus told this parable to his disciples: 'The kingdom of heaven will be like this: Ten bridesmaids took their lamps and went to meet the bridegroom. Five of them were foolish and five were sensible: the foolish ones did take their lamps, but they brought no oil, whereas the sensible ones took flasks of oil as well as their lamps. The bridegroom was late, and they all grew drowsy and fell asleep. But at midnight there was a cry, "The bridegroom is here! Go out and meet him." At this, all those bridesmaids woke up and trimmed their lamps, and the foolish ones said to the sensible ones, "Give us some of your oil: our lamps are going out." But they replied, "There may not be enough for us and for you; you had better go to those who sell it and buy some for yourselves." They had gone off to buy it when the bridegroom arrived. Those who were ready went in with him to the wedding hall and the door was closed. The other bridesmaids arrived later. "Lord, Lord," they said "open the door for us." But he replied, "I tell you solemnly, I do not know you." So stay awake, because you do not know either the day or the hour.'

The Gospel of the Lord.
Praise to you, Lord Jesus Christ.

▷ *page 11*

PRAYER OVER THE OFFERINGS

Look with favour, we pray, O Lord,
upon the sacrificial gifts offered here,
that, celebrating in mystery the Passion of your Son,
we may honour it with loving devotion.
Through Christ our Lord.   **Amen.**

▷ *page 15*

COMMUNION ANTIPHON   *cf Psalm 22:1–2*

The Lord is my shepherd; there is nothing I shall want.
Fresh and green are the pastures where he gives me repose,
near restful waters he leads me.

or   *cf Luke 24:35*

The disciples recognized the Lord Jesus in the breaking of bread.

▷ *page 58*

PRAYER AFTER COMMUNION

Nourished by this sacred gift, O Lord,
we give you thanks and beseech your mercy,
that, by the pouring forth of your Spirit,
the grace of integrity may endure
in those your heavenly power has entered.
Through Christ our Lord.   **Amen.**

▷ *page 59*

THIRTY-THIRD SUNDAY IN ORDINARY TIME

ENTRANCE ANTIPHON *Jeremiah 29:11, 12, 14*
The Lord said: I think thoughts of peace and not of affliction.
You will call upon me, and I will answer you,
and I will lead back your captives from every place.

▷ *page 7*

COLLECT
Grant us, we pray, O Lord our God,
the constant gladness of being devoted to you,
for it is full and lasting happiness
to serve with constancy
the author of all that is good.
Through our Lord Jesus Christ, your Son,
who lives and reigns with you in the unity of the Holy Spirit,
one God, for ever and ever. **Amen.**

ORDINARY

FIRST READING *Proverbs 31:10–13, 19–20, 30–31*
A perfect wife – who can find her?

A perfect wife – who can find her? She is far beyond the price of pearls. Her husband's heart has confidence in her, from her he will derive no little profit. Advantage and not hurt she brings him all the days of her life. She is always busy with wool and with flax, she does her work with eager hands. She sets her hand to the distaff, her fingers grasp the spindle. She holds out her hand to the poor, she opens her arms to the needy. Charm is deceitful, and beauty empty; the woman who is wise is the one to praise. Give her a share in what her hands have worked for, and let her works tell her praises at the city gates.

The word of the Lord.
Thanks be to God.

RESPONSORIAL PSALM *Psalm 127:1–5 Response v 1*

O blessed are those who fear the Lord.

1 O blessed are those who fear the Lord
   and walk in his ways!
   By the labour of your hands you shall eat.
   You will be happy and prosper.

2 Your wife like a fruitful vine
   in the heart of your house;
   your children like shoots of the olive,
   around your table.

3 Indeed thus shall be blessed
   the man who fears the Lord.
   May the Lord bless you from Zion
   in a happy Jerusalem
   all the days of your life!

SECOND READING   *1 Thessalonians 5:1–6*

Let not the Day of the Lord overtake you like a thief.

You will not be expecting us to write anything to you, brothers, about 'times and seasons', since you know very well that the Day of the Lord is going to come like a thief in the night. It is when people are saying, 'How quiet and peaceful it is' that the worst suddenly happens, as suddenly as labour pains come on a pregnant woman; and there will be no way for anybody to evade it.

But it is not as if you live in the dark, my brothers, for that Day to overtake you like a thief. No, you are all sons of light and sons of the day; we do not belong to the night or to darkness, so we should not go on sleeping, as everyone else does, but stay wide awake and sober.

The word of the Lord.
Thanks be to God.

GOSPEL ACCLAMATION   *Apocalypse 2:10*

> **Alleluia, alleluia!**
> **Even if you have to die, says the Lord,**
> **keep faithful, and I will give you**
> **the crown of life.**
> **Alleluia!**

or   *John 15:4, 5*

> **Alleluia, alleluia!**
> **Make your home in me, as I make mine in you,**
> **says the Lord.**
> **Whoever remains in me bears fruit in plenty.**
> **Alleluia!**

GOSPEL   *Matthew 25:14–30   Shorter form (omitting oblique text): Matthew 25:14–15, 19–20*

The Lord be with you.
And with your spirit.

A reading from the holy Gospel according to Matthew.
Glory to you, O Lord.

You have been faithful in small things; come and join in your master's happiness.

Jesus spoke this parable to his disciples: 'The kingdom of heaven is like a man on his way abroad who summoned his servants and entrusted his property to them. To one he gave five talents, to another two, to a third one; each in proportion to his ability. Then he set out. *The man who had received the five talents promptly went and traded with them and made five more. The man who had received two made two more in the same way. But the man who had received one went off and dug a hole in the* ground and hid his master's money. Now a long time after, the master of those servants came back and went through his accounts with them. The man who had received the five talents came forward bringing five more. "Sir," he said "you entrusted me with five talents; here are five more that I have made." His master said to him, "Well done, good and faithful servant; you have shown you can be faithful in small things, I will trust you with greater; come and join in your master's happiness." *Next the man with the two talents came forward. "Sir," he said, "you entrusted me with two talents; here are two more that I have made." His master said to him, "Well done, good and faithful servant; you have shown you can be faithful in small things, I will trust you with greater; come and join in your master's happiness." Last came forward the man who had the one talent. "Sir," said he, "I had heard you were a hard man, reaping where you have not sown and gathering where you have not scattered; so I was afraid, and I went off and hid your talent in the ground. Here it is; it was yours, you have it back." But his master answered him, "You wicked and lazy servant! So you knew that I reap where I have not sown and gather where I have not scattered? Well then, you should have deposited my money with the bankers, and on my return I would have recovered my capital with interest. So now, take the talent from him and give it to the man who has the five talents. For everyone who has will be given more, and he will have more than enough; but from the man who has not, even what he has will be taken away. As for this good-for-nothing servant, throw him out into the dark, where there will be weeping and grinding of teeth."'*

The Gospel of the Lord.
Praise to you, Lord Jesus Christ.

▷ page 11

PRAYER OVER THE OFFERINGS

Grant, O Lord, we pray,
that what we offer in the sight of your majesty
may obtain for us the grace of being devoted to you
and gain us the prize of everlasting happiness.
Through Christ our Lord.   **Amen.**

▷ page 15

COMMUNION ANTIPHON   *Psalm 72:28*

To be near God is my happiness,
to place my hope in God the Lord.

or   *Mark 11:23–24*

Amen, I say to you: Whatever you ask in prayer,
believe that you will receive,
and it shall be given to you, says the Lord.

▷ page 58

PRAYER AFTER COMMUNION

We have partaken of the gifts of this sacred mystery,
humbly imploring, O Lord,
that what your Son commanded us to do
in memory of him
may bring us growth in charity.
Through Christ our Lord.   **Amen.**

▷ page 59

OUR LORD JESUS CHRIST, KING OF THE UNIVERSE

ENTRANCE ANTIPHON   *Revelation 5:12; 1:6*

How worthy is the Lamb who was slain,
to receive power and divinity,
and wisdom and strength and honour.
To him belong glory and power for ever and ever.

▷ *page 7*

COLLECT

Almighty ever-living God,
whose will is to restore all things
in your beloved Son, the King of the universe,
grant, we pray,
that the whole creation, set free from slavery,
may render your majesty service
and ceaselessly proclaim your praise.
Through our Lord Jesus Christ, your Son,
who lives and reigns with you in the unity of the Holy Spirit,
one God, for ever and ever. **Amen.**

FIRST READING   *Ezekiel 34:11–12, 15–17*

As for you, my sheep, I will judge between sheep and sheep.

The Lord says this: I am going to look after my flock myself and keep all of it in view. As a shepherd keeps all his flock in view when he stands up in the middle of his scattered sheep, so shall I keep my sheep in view. I shall rescue them from wherever they have been scattered during the mist and darkness. I myself will pasture my sheep, I myself will show them where to rest – it is the Lord who speaks. I shall look for the lost one, bring back the stray, bandage the wounded and make the weak strong. I shall watch over the fat and healthy. I shall be a true shepherd to them.

As for you, my sheep, the Lord says this: I will judge between sheep and sheep, between rams and he-goats.

The word of the Lord.
Thanks be to God.

RESPONSORIAL PSALM   *Psalm 22:1–3, 5–6 response v 1*

**The Lord is my shepherd;
there is nothing I shall want.**

1   The Lord is my shepherd;
    there is nothing I shall want.
    Fresh and green are the pastures
    where he gives me repose.

2   Near restful waters he leads me,
    to revive my drooping spirit.
    He guides me along the right path;
    he is true to his name.

3   You have prepared a banquet for me
    in the sight of my foes.
    My head you have anointed with oil;
    my cup is overflowing.

4   Surely goodness and kindness shall follow me
    all the days of my life.
    In the Lord's own house shall I dwell
    for ever and ever.

SECOND READING   *1 Corinthians 15:20–26, 28*

He will hand over the kingdom to God the Father, so that God may be all in all.

Christ has been raised from the dead, the first-fruits of all who have fallen asleep. Death came through one man and in the same way the resurrection of the dead has come through one man. Just as all men die in Adam, so all men will be brought to life in Christ; but all of them in their proper order: Christ as the first-fruits and then, after the coming of Christ, those who belong to him. After that will come the end, when he hands over the kingdom to God the Father, having done away with every sovereignty, authority and power. For he must be king until he has put all his enemies under his feet and the last of the enemies to be destroyed is death. And when everything is subjected to him, then the Son himself will be subject in his turn to the One who subjected all things to him, so that God may be all in all.

The word of the Lord.
Thanks be to God.

GOSPEL ACCLAMATION   *Mark 11:10*

Alleluia, alleluia!
Blessings on him who comes in the name of the Lord!
Blessings on the coming kingdom of our father David!
Alleluia!

GOSPEL   *Matthew 25:31–46*

The Lord be with you.
And with your spirit.

A reading from the holy Gospel according to Matthew.
Glory to you, O Lord.

He will take his seat on his throne of glory, and he will separate men one from another.

Jesus said to his disciples: 'When the Son of Man comes in his glory, escorted by all the angels, then he will take his seat on his throne of glory. All the nations will be assembled before him and he will separate men one from another as the shepherd separates sheep from goats. He will place the sheep on his right hand and the goats on his left. Then the King will say to those on his right hand, "Come, you whom my Father has blessed, take for your heritage the kingdom prepared for you since the foundation of the world. For I was hungry and you gave me food; I was thirsty and you gave me drink; I was a stranger and you made me welcome; naked and you clothed me, sick and you visited me, in prison and you came to see me." Then the virtuous will say to him in reply, "Lord, when did we see you hungry and feed you; or thirsty and give you drink? When did we see you a stranger and make you welcome; naked and clothe you; sick or in prison and go to see you?" And the King will answer, "I tell you solemnly, in so far as you did this to one of the least of these brothers of mine, you did it to me." Next he will say to those on his left hand, "Go away from me, with your curse upon you, to the eternal fire prepared for the devil and his angels. For I was hungry and you never gave me food; I was thirsty and you never gave me anything to drink; I was a stranger and you never made me welcome, naked and you never clothed me, sick and in prison and you never visited me." Then it will be their turn to ask, "Lord, when did we see you hungry or thirsty, a stranger or naked, sick or in prison, and did not come to your help?" Then he will answer, "I tell you solemnly, in so far as you neglected to do this to one of the least of these, you neglected to do it to me." And they will go away to eternal punishment, and the virtuous to eternal life.'

The Gospel of the Lord.
Praise to you, Lord Jesus Christ.

▷ page 11

PRAYER OVER THE OFFERINGS

As we offer you, O Lord, the sacrifice
by which the human race is reconciled to you,
we humbly pray,
that your Son himself may bestow on all nations
the gifts of unity and peace.
Through Christ our Lord.   **Amen.**

▷ page 15

Preface: Christ, King of the Universe, page 68.

COMMUNION ANTIPHON   *Psalm 28:10–11*
The Lord sits as King for ever.
The Lord will bless his people with peace.

▷ page 58

PRAYER AFTER COMMUNION

Having received the food of immortality,
we ask, O Lord,
that, glorying in obedience
to the commands of Christ, the King of the universe,
we may live with him eternally in his heavenly Kingdom.
Who lives and reigns for ever and ever.   **Amen.**

▷ page 59

PROPER OF SAINTS

NATIVITY OF ST JOHN THE BAPTIST — VIGIL MASS

24 JUNE

If this Solemnity falls on a Sunday, it replaces the Sunday in Ordinary Time.
This Mass is used on the evening of 23 June.

ENTRANCE ANTIPHON *Luke 1:15, 14*

He will be great in the sight of the Lord
and will be filled with the Holy Spirit,
even from his mother's womb;
and many will rejoice at his birth.

▷ page 7

COLLECT

Grant, we pray, almighty God,
that your family may walk in the way of salvation
and, attentive to what Saint John the Precursor urged,
may come safely to the One he foretold,
our Lord Jesus Christ.
Who lives and reigns with you in the unity of the Holy Spirit,
one God, for ever and ever. **Amen.**

FIRST READING *Jeremiah 1:4–10*

Before I formed you in the womb, I knew you.

The word of the Lord was addressed to me, saying,

'Before I formed you in the womb I knew you; before you came to birth I consecrated you; I have appointed you as prophet to the nations.'

I said, 'Ah, Lord; look, I do not know how to speak: I am a child!' But the Lord replied,

'Do not say, "I am a child." Go now to those to whom I send you and say whatever I command you. Do not be afraid of them, for I am with you to protect you – it is the Lord who speaks!'

Then the Lord put out his hand and touched my mouth and said to me:

'There! I am putting my words into your mouth. Look, today I am setting you over nations and over kingdoms, to tear up and to knock down, to destroy and to overthrow, to build and to plant.'

The word of the Lord.
Thanks be to God.

RESPONSORIAL PSALM *Psalm 70:1–6, 15, 17 response v 6*

From my mother's womb you have been my help.

1 In you, O Lord, I take refuge:
   let me never be put to shame.
   In your justice rescue me, free me:
   pay heed to me and save me.

2 Be a rock where I can take refuge,
   a mighty stronghold to save me;
   for you are my rock, my stronghold.
   Free me from the hand of the wicked.

3   It is you, O Lord, who are my hope,
     my trust, O Lord, since my youth.
     On you I have leaned from my birth,
     from my mother's womb you have been my help.

4   My lips will tell of your justice
     and day by day of your help.
     O God, you have taught me from my youth
     and I proclaim your wonders still.

SECOND READING   *1 Peter 1:8–12*

It was this salvation that the prophets were looking and searching so hard for.

You did not see Jesus Christ, yet you love him; and still without seeing him, you are already filled with a joy so glorious that it cannot he described, because you believe; and you are sure of the end to which your faith looks forward, that is, the salvation of your souls.

It was this salvation that the prophets were looking and searching so hard for; their prophecies were about the grace which was to come to you. The Spirit of Christ which was in them foretold the sufferings of Christ and the glories that would come after them, and they tried to find out at what time and in what circumstances all this was to be expected. It was revealed to them that the news they brought of all the things which have now been announced to you, by those who preached to you the Good News through the Holy Spirit sent from heaven, was for you and not for themselves. Even the angels long to catch a glimpse of these things.

The word of the Lord.
Thanks be to God.

GOSPEL ACCLAMATION   *John 1:7; Luke 1:17*

Alleluia, alleluia!
He came as a witness,
to speak for the light,
preparing for the Lord a people fit for him
Alleluia!

GOSPEL   *Luke 1:5–17*

The Lord be with you.
And with your spirit.

A reading from the holy Gospel according to Luke.
Glory to you, O Lord.

She is to bear you a son and you must name him John.

In the days of King Herod of Judaea there lived a priest called Zechariah who belonged to the Abijah section of the priesthood, and he had a wife, Elizabeth by name, who was a descendant of Aaron. Both were worthy in the sight of God, and scrupulously observed all the commandments and observances of the Lord. But they were childless: Elizabeth was barren and they were both getting on in years.

Now it was the turn of Zechariah's section to serve, and he was exercising his priestly office before God when it fell to him by lot, as the ritual custom was, to enter the Lord's sanctuary and burn incense there. And at the hour of incense the whole congregation was outside, praying.

Then there appeared to him the angel of the Lord, standing on the right of the altar of incense. The sight disturbed Zechariah and he was overcome with fear. But the angel said to him, 'Zechariah, do not be afraid, your prayer has been heard. Your wife Elizabeth is to bear you a son and you must name him John. He will be your joy and delight and many will rejoice at his birth, for he will be great in the sight of the Lord; he must drink no wine, no strong drink. Even from his mother's womb he will be filled with the Holy Spirit, and he will bring back many of the sons of Israel to the Lord their God. With the spirit and power of Elijah, he will go before him to turn the hearts of fathers towards their children and the disobedient back to the wisdom that the virtuous have, preparing for the Lord a people fit for him.'

The Gospel of the Lord.
Praise to you, Lord Jesus Christ.

▷ page 11

PROFESSION OF FAITH
The Profession of Faith is said.

PRAYER OVER THE OFFERINGS
Look with favour, O Lord,
upon the offerings made by your people
on the Solemnity of Saint John the Baptist,
and grant that what we celebrate in mystery
we may follow with deeds of devoted service.
Through Christ our Lord.   **Amen.**

▷ page 15

Preface: The mission of the Precursor, page 69.

COMMUNION ANTIPHON   *Luke 1:68*
Blessed be the Lord, the God of Israel!
He has visited his people and redeemed them.

▷ page 58

PRAYER AFTER COMMUNION
May the marvellous prayer of Saint John the Baptist
accompany us who have eaten our fill
at this sacrificial feast, O Lord,
and, since Saint John proclaimed your Son
to be the Lamb who would take away our sins,
may he implore now for us your favour.
Through Christ our Lord.   **Amen.**

▷ page 59

NATIVITY OF ST JOHN THE BAPTIST – MASS DURING THE DAY

24 JUNE

If this Solemnity falls on a Sunday, it replaces the Sunday in Ordinary Time.

ENTRANCE ANTIPHON   *John 1: 6–7; Luke 1:17*

A man was sent from God, whose name was John.
He came to testify to the light,
to prepare a people fit for the Lord.

▷ *page 7*

COLLECT

O God, who raised up Saint John the Baptist
to make ready a nation fit for Christ the Lord,
give your people, we pray,
the grace of spiritual joys
and direct the hearts of all the faithful
into the way of salvation and peace.
Through our Lord Jesus Christ, your Son,
who lives and reigns with you in the unity of the Holy Spirit,
one God, for ever and ever.   **Amen.**

FIRST READING   *Isaiah 49:1–6*

I will make you the light of the nations.

Islands, listen to me, pay attention remotest peoples. The Lord called me before I was born, from my mother's womb he pronounced my name.

He made my mouth a sharp sword, and hid me in the shadow of his hand. He made me into a sharpened arrow. and concealed me in his quiver.

He said to me, 'You are my servant (Israel) in whom I shall be glorified'; while I was thinking, 'I have toiled in vain, I have exhausted myself for nothing':

and all the while my cause was with the Lord, my reward with my God. I was honoured in the eyes of the Lord, my God was my strength.

And now the Lord has spoken, he who formed me in the womb to be his servant, to bring Jacob back to him, to gather Israel to him:

'It is not enough for you to be my servant, to restore the tribes of Jacob and bring back the survivors of Israel; I will make you the light of the nations so that my salvation may reach to the ends of the earth.'

The word of the Lord.
Thanks be to God.

RESPONSORIAL PSALM   *Psalm 138:1–3, 13–15 response v 14*

I thank you for the wonder of my being.

1   O Lord, you search me and you know me,
   you know my resting and my rising,
   you discern my purpose from afar.
   You mark when I walk or lie down,
   all my ways lie open to you.

continued...

SAINTS

I thank you for the wonder of my being.

2   For it was you who created my being,
     knit me together in my mother's womb.
     I thank you for the wonder of my being,
     for the wonders of all your creation.

3   Already you knew my soul,
     my body held no secret from you
     when I was being fashioned in secret
     and moulded in the depths of the earth.

SECOND READING   *Acts 13:22–26*

Jesus, whose coming was heralded by John.

Paul said: 'God made David the king of our ancestors, of whom he approved in these words. "I have selected David son of Jesse, a man after my own heart, who will carry out my whole purpose." To keep his promise, God has raised up for Israel one of David's descendants, Jesus, as Saviour, whose coming was heralded by John when he proclaimed a baptism of repentance for the whole people of Israel. Before John ended his career he said, "I am not the one you imagine me to be; that one is coming after me and I am not fit to undo his sandal."

'My brothers, sons of Abraham's race, and all you who fear God, this message of salvation is meant for you.'

The word of the Lord.
Thanks be to God.

GOSPEL ACCLAMATION   *cf Luke 1:76*

**Alleluia, alleluia!
As for you, little child, you shall be called
a prophet of God, the Most High.
You shall go ahead of the Lord
to prepare his ways before him.
Alleluia!**

GOSPEL   *Luke 1:57–66, 80*

The Lord be with you.
And with your spirit.

A reading from the holy Gospel according to Luke.
Glory to you, O Lord.

His name is John.

The time came for Elizabeth to have her child, and she gave birth to a son; and when her neighbours and relations heard that the Lord had shown her so great a kindness, they shared her joy.

Now on the eighth day they came to circumcise the child; they were going to call him Zechariah after his father, but his mother spoke up. 'No,' she said 'he is to be called John.' They said to her, 'But no one in your family has that name', and made signs to his father to find out what he wanted him called. The father asked for a writing tablet and wrote, 'His name is John.' And they were all astonished. At that instant his power of speech returned and he spoke and praised God. All their neighbours were filled with awe and the whole affair was talked about throughout the hill country of Judaea. All those who heard of it treasured it in their hearts. 'What will this child turn out to be?' they wondered. And indeed the hand of the Lord was with him. The child grew up and his spirit matured. And he lived out in the wilderness until the day he appeared openly to Israel.

The Gospel of the Lord.
Praise to you, Lord Jesus Christel.

▷ *page 11*

PROFESSION OF FAITH
The Profession of Faith is said.

PRAYER OVER THE OFFERINGS
We place these offerings on your altar, O Lord,
to celebrate with fitting honour the nativity of him
who both foretold the coming of the world's Saviour
and pointed him out when he came.
Who lives and reigns for ever and ever.   **Amen.**

▷ *page 15*

Preface: The mission of the Precursor, page 69.

COMMUNION ANTIPHON   *cf Luke 1:78*
Through the tender mercy of our God,
the Dawn from on high will visit us.

▷ *page 58*

PRAYER AFTER COMMUNION
Having feasted at the banquet of the heavenly Lamb,
we pray, O Lord,
that, finding joy in the nativity of Saint John the Baptist,
your Church may know as the author of her rebirth
the Christ whose coming John foretold.
Who lives and reigns for ever and ever.   **Amen.**

▷ *page 59*

SS PETER AND PAUL, APOSTLES — VIGIL MASS

29 JUNE

This Mass is used on the evening before the Solemnity.

If this Solemnity falls on a Sunday, it replaces the Sunday in Ordinary Time.
In certain territories, this Solemnity may be transferred to the nearest Sunday,
replacing the Sunday in Ordinary Time.

ENTRANCE ANTIPHON
Peter the Apostle, and Paul the teacher of the Gentiles,
these have taught us your law, O Lord.

▷ *page 7*

COLLECT

Grant, we pray, O Lord our God,
that we may be sustained
by the intercession of the blessed Apostles Peter and Paul,
that, as through them you gave your Church
the foundations of her heavenly office,
so through them you may help her to eternal salvation.
Through our Lord Jesus Christ, your Son,
who lives and reigns with you in the unity of the Holy Spirit,
one God, for ever and ever. **Amen.**

FIRST READING   *Acts 3:1–10*

I will give you what I have: in the name of Jesus stand up and walk!

Once, when Peter and John were going up to the Temple for the prayers at the ninth hour, it happened that there was a man being carried past. He was a cripple from birth; and they used to put him down every day near the Temple entrance called the Beautiful Gate so that he could beg from the people going in. When this man saw Peter and John on their way into the Temple he begged from them. Both Peter and John looked straight at him and said, 'Look at us.' He turned to them expectantly, hoping to get something from them, but Peter said, 'I have neither silver nor gold, but I will give you what I have: in the name of Jesus Christ the Nazarene, walk!' Peter then took him by the hand and helped him to stand up. Instantly his feet and ankles became firm, he jumped up, stood, and began to walk, and he went with them into the Temple, walking and jumping and praising God. Everyone could see him walking and praising God, and they recognised him as the man who used to sit begging at the Beautiful Gate of the Temple. They were all astonished and unable to explain what had happened to him.

The word of the Lord.
Thanks be to God.

RESPONSORIAL PSALM   *Psalm 18:2–5 response v 5*

Their word goes forth through all the earth.

1 The heavens proclaim the glory of God
and the firmament shows forth the work of his hands.
Day unto day takes up the story
and night unto night makes known the message.

2 No speech, no word, no voice is heard
yet their span extends through all the earth,
their words to the utmost bounds of the world.

SECOND READING   *Galatians 1:11–20*

God specially chose me while I was still in my mother's womb.

The Good News I preached is not a human message that I was given by men, it is something I learnt only through a revelation of Jesus Christ. You must have heard of my career as a practising Jew, how merciless I was in persecuting the Church of God, how much damage I did to it, how I stood out among other Jews of my generation, and how enthusiastic I was for the traditions of my ancestors.

Then God, who had specially chosen me while I was still in my mother's womb, called me through his grace and chose to reveal his Son to me, so that I might preach the Good News about him to the pagans. I did not stop to discuss this with any human being, nor did I go up to Jerusalem to see those who were already apostles before me, but I went off to Arabia at once and later went straight back from there to Damascus. Even when after three years I went up to Jerusalem to visit Cephas and stayed with him for fifteen days, I did not see any of the other apostles; I only saw James, the brother of the Lord, and I swear before God that what I have just written is the literal truth.

The word of the Lord.
Thanks be to God.

GOSPEL ACCLAMATION   *John 21:17*

Alleluia, alleluia!
Lord, you know everything;
you know I love you.
Alleluia!

GOSPEL   *John 21:15–19*

The Lord be with you.
And with your spirit.

A reading from the holy Gospel according to John.
Glory to you, O Lord.

Feed my lambs, feed my sheep.

After Jesus had shown himself to his disciples and eaten with them, he said to Simon Peter, 'Simon son of John, do you love me more than these others do?' He answered, 'Yes, Lord, you know I love you.' Jesus said to him, 'Feed my lambs.' A second time he said to him, 'Simon son of John, do you love me?' He replied, 'Yes, Lord, you know I love you.' Jesus said to him, 'Look after my sheep.' Then he said to him a third time, 'Simon son of John, do you love me?' Peter was upset that he asked him the third time, 'Do you love me?' and said, 'Lord, you know everything; you know I love you.' Jesus said to him, 'Feed my sheep.

'I tell you most solemnly, when you were young you put on your own belt and walked where you liked; but when you grow old you will stretch out your hands, and somebody else will put a belt round you and take you where you would rather not go.'

In these words he indicated the kind of death by which Peter would give glory to God. After this he said, 'Follow me.'

The Gospel of the Lord.
Praise to you, Lord Jesus Christ.

▷ *page 11*

PROFESSION OF FAITH
The Profession of Faith is said.

PRAYER OVER THE OFFERINGS

We bring offerings to your altar, O Lord,
as we glory in the solemn feast
of the blessed Apostles Peter and Paul,
so that the more we doubt our own merits,
the more we may rejoice that we are to be saved
by your loving kindness.
Through Christ our Lord.   **Amen.**

▷ page 15

Preface: The twofold mission of Peter and Paul in the Church, page 69.

COMMUNION ANTIPHON   *cf John 21:15, 17*

Simon, Son of John, do you love me more than these?
Lord, you know everything; you know that I love you.

▷ page 58

PRAYER AFTER COMMUNION

By this heavenly Sacrament, O Lord, we pray,
strengthen your faithful,
whom you have enlightened with the teaching of the Apostles.
Through Christ our Lord.   **Amen.**

▷ page 59

A solemn blessing may be used.

SS PETER AND PAUL, APOSTLES — MASS DURING THE DAY

*If this Solemnity falls on a Sunday, it replaces the Sunday in Ordinary Time.
In certain territories, this Solemnity may be transferred to the nearest Sunday,
replacing the Sunday in Ordinary Time.*

ENTRANCE ANTIPHON

These are the ones who, living in the flesh,
planted the Church with their blood;
they drank the chalice of the Lord
and became the friends of God.

▷ page 7

COLLECT

O God, who on the Solemnity of the Apostles Peter and Paul
give us the noble and holy joy of this day,
grant, we pray, that your Church
may in all things follow the teaching
of those through whom she received
the beginnings of right religion.
Through our Lord Jesus Christ, your Son,
who lives and reigns with you in the unity of the Holy Spirit,
one God, for ever and ever.   **Amen.**

FIRST READING   *Acts 12:1–11*

Now I know the Lord really did save me from Herod.

King Herod started persecuting certain members of the Church. He beheaded James the brother of John, and when he saw that this pleased the Jews he decided to arrest Peter as well. This was during the days of Unleavened Bread, and he put Peter in prison, assigning four squads of four soldiers each to guard him in turns. Herod meant to try Peter in public after the end of the Passover week. All the time Peter was under guard the Church prayed to God for him unremittingly.

On the night before Herod was to try him, Peter was sleeping between two soldiers, fastened with double chains, while guards kept watch at the main entrance to the prison. Then suddenly the angel of the Lord stood there, and the cell was filled with light. He tapped Peter on the side and woke him. 'Get up!' he said 'Hurry!' – and the chains fell from his hands. The angel then said, 'Put on your belt and sandals.' After he had done this, the angel next said, 'Wrap your cloak round you and follow me.' Peter followed him, but had no idea that what the angel did was all happening in reality; he thought he was seeing a vision. They passed through two guard posts one after the other, and reached the iron gate leading to the city. This opened of its own accord; they went through it and had walked the whole length of one street when suddenly the angel left him. It was only then that Peter came to himself. 'Now I know it is all true,' he said. 'The Lord really did send his angel and has saved me from Herod and from all that the Jewish people were so certain would happen to me.'

The word of the Lord.
Thanks be to God.

SAINTS

RESPONSORIAL PSALM   *Psalm 33:2–9 response v 5; alternative response v 8*

From all my terrors the Lord set me free.

or

The angel of the Lord rescues those who revere him.

1 I will bless the Lord at all times,
   his praise always on my lips;
   in the Lord my soul shall make its boast.
   The humble shall hear and be glad.

2 Glorify the Lord with me.
   Together let us praise his name
   I sought the Lord and he answered me;
   from all my terrors he set me free.

3 Look towards him and be radiant;
   let your faces not be at ashed.
   This poor man called; the Lord heard him
   and rescued him from all his distress.

4 The angel of the Lord is encamped
   around those who revere him, to rescue them.
   Taste and see that the Lord is good.
   He is happy who seeks refuge in him.

SECOND READING   *2 Timothy 4:6–8, 17–18*

All there is to come now is the crown of righteousness reserved for me.

My life is already being poured away as a libation, and the time has come for me to be gone. I have fought the good fight to the end; I have run the race to the finish; I have kept the faith; all there is to come now is the crown of righteousness reserved for me, which the Lord, the righteous judge, will give to me on that Day; and not only to me but to all those who have longed for his Appearing.

The Lord stood by me and gave me power, so that through me the whole message might be proclaimed for all the pagans to hear; and so I was rescued from the lion's mouth. The Lord will rescue me from all evil attempts on me, and bring me safely to his heavenly kingdom. To him be glory for ever and ever. Amen.

The word of the Lord.
Thanks be to God.

GOSPEL ACCLAMATION   *Matthew 16:18*

Alleluia, alleluia!
You are Peter and on this rock I will build my Church.
And the gates of the underworld can never hold out against it.
Alleluia!

GOSPEL   *Matthew 16:13–19*

The Lord be with you.
And with your spirit.

A reading from the holy Gospel according to Matthew.
Glory to you, O Lord.

You are Peter, and I will give you the keys of the kingdom of heaven.

When Jesus came to the region of Caesarea Philippi he put this question to his disciples, 'Who do people say the Son of Man is?' And they said, 'Some say he is John the Baptist, some Elijah, and others Jeremiah or one of the prophets.' 'But you,' he said, 'who do you say I am?' Then Simon Peter spoke up. 'You are the Christ,' he said 'the Son of the living God.' Jesus replied, 'Simon son of Jonah, you are a happy man! Because it was not flesh and blood that revealed this to you but my Father in heaven. So I now say to you: You are Peter and on this rock I will build my Church. And the gates of the underworld can never hold out against it. I will give you the keys of the kingdom of heaven: whatever you bind on earth shall be considered bound in heaven; whatever you loose on earth shall be considered loosed in heaven.'

The Gospel of the Lord.
Praise to you, Lord Jesus Christ.

▷ *page 11*

PROFESSION OF FAITH
The Profession of Faith is said.

PRAYER OVER THE OFFERINGS

May the prayer of the Apostles, O Lord,
accompany the sacrificial gift
that we present to your name for consecration,
and may their intercession make us devoted to you
in celebration of the sacrifice.
Through Christ our Lord. **Amen.**

▷ page 15

Preface: The twofold mission of Peter and Paul in the Church, page 69.

COMMUNION ANTIPHON   *cf Matthew 16:16, 18*

Peter said to Jesus: You are the Christ, the Son of the living God.
And Jesus replied: You are Peter,
and upon this rock I will build my Church.

▷ page 58

PRAYER AFTER COMMUNION

Grant us, O Lord,
who have been renewed by this Sacrament,
so to live in the Church,
that, persevering in the breaking of the Bread
and in the teaching of the Apostles,
we may be one heart and one soul,
made steadfast in your love.
Through Christ our Lord. **Amen.**

▷ page 59

A solemn blessing may be used.

TRANSFIGURATION OF THE LORD

6 AUGUST
If this feast falls on a Sunday, it replaces the Sunday in Ordinary Time.
When the Feast is celebrated on a weekday there is only one reading before the Gospel.

ENTRANCE ANTIPHON   *cf Matthew 17:5*

In a resplendent cloud the Holy Spirit appeared.
The Father's voice was heard: This is my beloved Son,
with whom I am well pleased. Listen to him.

▷ page 7

COLLECT

O God, who in the glorious Transfiguration
of your Only Begotten Son
confirmed the mysteries of faith by the witness of the Fathers
and wonderfully prefigured our full adoption to sonship,
grant, we pray, to your servants,
that, listening to the voice of your beloved Son,
we may merit to become coheirs with him.
Who lives and reigns with you in the unity of the Holy Spirit,
one God, for ever and ever. **Amen.**

FIRST READING *Daniel 7:9–10, 13–14*

His robe was white as snow.

As I watched: Thrones were set in place and one of great age took his seat. His robe was white as snow, the hair of his head as pure as wool. His throne was a blaze of flames, its wheels were a burning fire. A stream of fire poured out, issuing from his presence. A thousand thousand waited on him, ten thousand times ten thousand stood before him. A court was held and the books were opened. I gazed into the visions of the night. And I saw, coming on the clouds of heaven, one like a son of man. He came to the one of great age and was led into his presence. On him was conferred sovereignty, glory and kingship, and men of all peoples, nations and languages became his servants. His sovereignty is an eternal sovereignty which shall never pass away, nor will his empire ever be destroyed.

The word of the Lord.
Thanks be to God.

RESPONSORIAL PSALM *Psalm 96:1–2, 5–6, 9 response vv 1, 9*

**The Lord is king,
most high above all the earth.**

1 The Lord is king, let earth rejoice,
let all the coastlands be glad.
Cloud and darkness are his raiment;
his throne, justice and right.

2 The mountains melt like wax
before the Lord of all the earth.
The skies proclaim his justice;
all peoples see his glory.

3 For you indeed are the Lord
most high above all the earth
exalted far above all spirits.

SECOND READING *2 Peter 1:16–19*

We heard this ourselves, spoken from heaven.

It was not any cleverly invented myths that we were repeating when we brought you the knowledge of the power and the coming of our Lord Jesus Christ; we had seen his majesty for ourselves. He was honoured and glorified by God the Father, when the Sublime Glory itself spoke to him and said, 'This is my Son, the Beloved; he enjoys my favour.' We heard this ourselves, spoken from heaven, when we were with him on the holy mountain.

So we have confirmation of what was said in prophecies; and you will be right to depend on prophecy and take it as a lamp for lighting a way through the dark until the dawn comes and the morning star rises in your minds.

The word of the Lord.
Thanks be to God.

GOSPEL ACCLAMATION *Matthew 17:5*

**Alleluia, alleluia!
This is my Son, the Beloved,
he enjoys my favour;
listen to him.
Alleluia!**

GOSPEL   *Matthew 17:1–9*

The Lord be with you.
And with your spirit.

A reading from the holy Gospel according to Matthew.
Glory to you, O Lord.

His face shone like the sun.

Jesus took with him Peter and James and his brother John and led them up a high mountain where they could be alone. There in their presence he was transfigured: his face shone like the sun and his clothes became as white as the light. Suddenly Moses and Elijah appeared to them; they were talking with him. Then Peter spoke to Jesus. 'Lord,' he said 'it is wonderful for us to be here; if you wish, I will make three tents here, one for you, one for Moses and one for Elijah.' He was still speaking when suddenly a bright cloud covered them with shadow, and from the cloud there came a voice which said, 'This is my Son; the Beloved; he enjoys my favour. Listen to him.' When they heard this, the disciples fell on their faces, overcome with fear. But Jesus came up and touched them. 'Stand up,' he said 'do not be afraid.' And when they raised their eyes they saw no one but only Jesus.

As they came down from the mountain Jesus gave them this order. 'Tell no one about the vision until the Son of Man has risen from the dead.'

The Gospel of the Lord.
Praise to you, Lord Jesus Christ.

▷ *page 11*

PROFESSION OF FAITH
The Profession of Faith is said when this feast is celebrated on Sunday.

PRAYER OVER THE OFFERINGS
Sanctify, O Lord, we pray,
these offerings here made to celebrate
the glorious Transfiguration of your Only Begotten Son,
and by his radiant splendour
cleanse us from the stains of sin.
Through Christ our Lord.   **Amen.**

▷ *page 15*

Preface: The Mystery of the Transfiguration, page 70.

COMMUNION ANTIPHON   *cf 1 John 3:2*
When Christ appears, we shall be like him,
for we shall see him as he is.

▷ *page 58*

PRAYER AFTER COMMUNION
May the heavenly nourishment we have received,
O Lord, we pray,
transform us into the likeness of your Son,
whose radiant splendour you willed to make manifest
in his glorious Transfiguration.
Who lives and reigns for ever and ever.   **Amen.**

▷ *page 59*

SAINTS

ASSUMPTION OF THE BLESSED VIRGIN — VIGIL MASS

ASSUMPTION OF THE BLESSED VIRGIN MARY
15 AUGUST

This Mass is used on the evening before the Solemnity.

If this Solemnity falls on a Sunday, it replaces the Sunday in Ordinary Time.
In certain territories, this Solemnity may be transferred to the nearest Sunday,
replacing the Sunday in Ordinary Time.

ENTRANCE ANTIPHON
Glorious things are spoken of you, O Mary,
who today were exalted above the choirs of Angels
into eternal triumph with Christ.

▷ page 7

COLLECT
O God, who, looking on the lowliness of the Blessed Virgin Mary,
raised her to this grace,
that your Only Begotten Son was born of her according to the flesh
and that she was crowned this day with surpassing glory,
grant through her prayers,
that, saved by the mystery of your redemption,
we may merit to be exalted by you on high.
Through our Lord Jesus Christ, your Son,
who lives and reigns with you in the unity of the Holy Spirit,
one God, for ever and ever. **Amen.**

FIRST READING *1 Chronicles 15:3–4, 15–16; 16:1–2*
They brought in the ark of God and set it inside the tent which David had pitched for it.

David gathered all Israel together in Jerusalem to bring the ark of God up to the place he had prepared for it. David called together the sons of Aaron and the sons of Levi. And the Levites carried the ark of God with the shafts on their shoulders, as Moses had ordered in accordance with the word of the Lord.

David then told the heads of the Levites to assign duties for their kinsmen as cantors, with their various instruments of music, harps and lyres and cymbals, to play joyful tunes. They brought the ark of God in and put it inside the tent that David had pitched for it: and they offered holocausts before God, and communion sacrifices. And when David had finished offering holocausts and communion sacrifices, he blessed the people in the name of the Lord.

The word of the Lord.
Thanks be to God.

RESPONSORIAL PSALM   *Psalm 131:6–7, 9–10, 13–14 response v 8*

Go up, Lord, to the place of your rest,
you and the ark of your strength.

1   At Ephrata we heard of the ark;
    we found it in the plains of Yearim.
    'Let us go to the place of his dwelling;
    let us go to kneel at his footstool.'

2   Your priests shall be clothed with holiness:
    your faithful shall ring out their joy.
    For the sake of David your servant
    do not reject your anointed.

3   For the Lord has chosen Zion;
    he has desired it for his dwelling:
    'This is my resting-place for ever,
    here have I chosen to live.'

SECOND READING   *1 Corinthians 15:54–57*

He gave us victory through our Lord Jesus Christ.

When this perishable nature has put on imperishability, and when this mortal nature has put on immortality, then the words of scripture will come true: Death is swallowed up in victory. Death, where is your victory? Death, where is your sting? Now the sting of death is sin and sin gets its power from the Law. So let us thank God for giving us the victory through our Lord Jesus Christ.

The word of the Lord.
Thanks be to God.

GOSPEL ACCLAMATION   *Luke 11:28*

Alleluia, alleluia!
Happy are those
who hear the word of God,
and keep it.
Alleluia!

GOSPEL   *Luke 11:27–28*

The Lord be with you.
And with your spirit.

A reading from the holy Gospel according to Luke.
Glory to you, O Lord.

Happy the womb that bore you

As Jesus was speaking, a woman in the crowd raised her voice and said, 'Happy the womb that bore you and the breasts you sucked!' But he replied, 'Still happier those who hear the word of God and keep it!'

The Gospel of the Lord.
Praise to you, Lord Jesus Christ.

▷ *page 11*

PROFESSION OF FAITH
The Profession of Faith is said.

PRAYER OVER THE OFFERINGS
Receive, we pray, O Lord,
the sacrifice of conciliation and praise,
which we celebrate on the Assumption of the holy Mother of God,
that it may lead us to your pardon
and confirm us in perpetual thanksgiving.
Through Christ our Lord.   **Amen.**

▷ *page 15*

Preface: The Glory of Mary assumed into heaven, page 70.

COMMUNION ANTIPHON   *cf Luke 11:27*
Blessed is the womb of the Virgin Mary,
which bore the Son of the eternal Father.

▷ *page 58*

PRAYER AFTER COMMUNION
Having partaken of this heavenly table,
we beseech your mercy, Lord our God,
that we, who honour the Assumption of the Mother of God,
may be freed from every threat of harm.
Through Christ our Lord.   **Amen.**

▷ *page 59*

A solemn blessing may be used.

ASSUMPTION OF THE BLESSED VIRGIN — DURING THE DAY

ASSUMPTION OF THE BLESSED VIRGIN MARY
15 AUGUST

If this Solemnity falls on a Sunday, it replaces the Sunday in Ordinary Time.
In certain territories, this Solemnity may be transferred to the nearest Sunday,
replacing the Sunday in Ordinary Time.

ENTRANCE ANTIPHON   *cf Revelation 12:1*
A great sign appeared in heaven:
a woman clothed with the sun, and the moon beneath her feet,
and on her head a crown of twelve stars.
or

Let us all rejoice in the Lord,
as we celebrate the feast day in honour of the Virgin Mary,
at whose Assumption the Angels rejoice
and praise the Son of God.

▷ *page 7*

COLLECT

Almighty ever-living God,
who assumed the Immaculate Virgin Mary, the Mother of your Son,
body and soul into heavenly glory,
grant, we pray,
that, always attentive to the things that are above,
we may merit to be sharers of her glory.
Through our Lord Jesus Christ, your Son,
who lives and reigns with you in the unity of the Holy Spirit,
one God, for ever and ever.   **Amen.**

FIRST READING   *Apocalypse 11:19; 12:1–6, 10*

A woman adorned with the sun, standing on the moon.

The sanctuary of God in heaven opened, and the ark of the covenant could be seen inside it.

Now a great sign appeared in heaven: a woman, adorned with the sun, standing on the moon, and with the twelve stars on her head for a crown. She was pregnant, and in labour, crying aloud in the pangs of childbirth. Then a second sign appeared in the sky, a huge red dragon which had seven heads and ten horns, and each of the seven heads crowned with a coronet. Its tail dragged a third of the stars from the sky and dropped them to the earth, and the dragon stopped in front of the woman as she was having the child, so that he could eat it as soon as it was born from its mother. The woman brought a male child into the world, the son who was to rule all the nations with an iron sceptre, and the child was taken straight up to God and to his throne, while the woman escaped into the desert, where God had made a place of safety ready. Then I heard a voice shout from heaven. 'Victory and power and empire for ever have been won by our God, and all authority for his Christ.'

The word of the Lord.
Thanks be to God.

RESPONSORIAL PSALM   *Psalm 44:10–12, 16 response v 10*

**On your right stands the queen,
in garments of gold.**

1   The daughters of kings are among your loved ones.
    On your right stands the queen in gold of Ophir.
    Listen, O daughter, give ear to my words:
    forget your own people and your father's house.

2   So will the king desire your beauty:
    he is your lord, pay homage to him.
    They are escorted amid gladness and joy;
    they pass within the palace of the king.

SECOND READING   *1 Corinthians 15:20–26*

Christ as the first-fruits and then, those who belong to him.

Christ has been raised from the dead, the first-fruits of all who have fallen asleep. Death came through one man and in the same way the resurrection of the dead has come through one man. Just as all men die in Adam, so all men will be brought to life in Christ; but all of them in their proper order: Christ as the first-fruits and then, after the coming of Christ, those who belong to him. After that will come the end, when he hands over the kingdom to God the Father, having done away with every sovereignty, authority and power. For he must be king until he has put all his enemies under his feet and the last of the enemies to be destroyed is death, for everything is to be put under his feet.

The word of the Lord.
Thanks be to God.

GOSPEL ACCLAMATION

Alleluia, alleluia!
Mary has been taken up into heaven;
all the choirs of angels are rejoicing.
Alleluia!

GOSPEL   *Luke 1:39–56*

The Lord be with you.
And with your spirit.

A reading from the holy Gospel according to Luke.
Glory to you, O Lord.

The Almighty has done great things for me, he has exalted the lowly.

Mary set out and went as quickly as she could to a town in the hill country of Judah. She went into Zechariah's house and greeted Elizabeth. Now as soon as Elizabeth heard Mary's greeting, the child leapt in her womb and Elizabeth was filled with the Holy Spirit. She gave a loud cry and said, 'Of all women you are the most blessed, and blessed is the fruit of your womb. Why should I be honoured with a visit from the mother of my Lord? For the moment your greeting reached my ears, the child in my womb leapt for joy. Yes, blessed is she who believed that the promise made her by the Lord would be fulfilled.'

And Mary said:

'My soul proclaims the greatness of the Lord and my spirit exults in God my saviour; because he has looked upon his lowly handmaid. Yes, from this day forward all generations will call me blessed, for the Almighty has done great things for me. Holy is his name, and his mercy reaches from age to age for those who fear him. He has shown the power of his arm, he has routed the proud of heart. He has pulled down princes from their thrones and exalted the lowly. The hungry he has filled with good things, the rich sent empty away. He has come to the help of Israel his servant, mindful of his mercy – according to the promise he made to our ancestors – of his mercy to Abraham and to his descendants for ever.'

Mary stayed with Elizabeth about three months and then went back home.

The Gospel of the Lord.
Praise to you, Lord Jesus Christ.

▷ page 11

PROFESSION OF FAITH
The Profession of Faith is said.

PRAYER OVER THE OFFERINGS
May this oblation, our tribute of homage,
rise up to you, O Lord,
and, through the intercession of the most Blessed Virgin Mary,
whom you assumed into heaven,
may our hearts, aflame with the fire of love,
constantly long for you.
Through Christ our Lord. **Amen.**

▷ *page 15*

Preface: The Glory of Mary assumed into heaven, page 70.

COMMUNION ANTIPHON   *Luke 1:48–49*
All generations will call me blessed,
for he who is mighty has done great things for me.

▷ *page 58*

PRAYER AFTER COMMUNION
Having received the Sacrament of salvation,
we ask you to grant, O Lord,
that, through the intercession of the Blessed Virgin Mary,
whom you assumed into heaven,
we may be brought to the glory of the resurrection.
Through Christ our Lord. **Amen.**

▷ *page 59*

A solemn blessing may be used.

EXALTATION OF THE HOLY CROSS

14 SEPTEMBER
If this feast falls on a Sunday, it replaces the Sunday in Ordinary Time.
When the Feast is celebrated on a weekday there is only one reading before the Gospel.

ENTRANCE ANTIPHON   *cf Galatians 6:14*
We should glory in the Cross of our Lord Jesus Christ,
in whom is our salvation, life and resurrection,
through whom we are saved and delivered.

▷ *page 7*

COLLECT
O God, who willed that your Only Begotten Son
should undergo the Cross to save the human race,
grant, we pray,
that we, who have known his mystery on earth,
may merit the grace of his redemption in heaven.
Through our Lord Jesus Christ, your Son,
who lives and reigns with you in the unity of the Holy Spirit,
one God, for ever and ever. **Amen.**

FIRST READING   *Numbers 21:4–9*

If anyone was bitten by a serpent, he looked at the bronze serpent and lived.

On the way through the wilderness, the Israelites lost patience. They spoke against God and against Moses. 'Why did you bring us out of Egypt to die in this wilderness? For there is neither bread nor water here: we are sick of this unsatisfying food.'

At this God sent fiery serpents among the people; their bite brought death to many in Israel. The people came and said to Moses, 'We have sinned by speaking against the Lord and against you. Intercede for us with the Lord to save us from these serpents.' Moses interceded for the people, and the Lord answered him, 'Make a fiery serpent and put it on a standard. If anyone is bitten and looks at it he shall live.' So Moses fashioned a bronze serpent which he put on a standard, and if anyone was bitten by a serpent, he looked at the bronze serpent and lived.

The word of the Lord.
Thanks be to God.

RESPONSORIAL PSALM   *Psalm 77:1–2, 34–38 response v 7*

Never forget the deeds of the Lord.

1 Give heed, my people, to my teaching;
   turn your ear to the words of my mouth.
   I will open my mouth in a parable
   and reveal hidden lessons of the past.

2 When he slew them then they would seek him,
   return and seek him in earnest.
   They would remember that God was their rock,
   God the Most High their redeemer.

3 But the words they spoke were mere flattery;
   they lied to him with their lips.
   For their hearts were not truly with him;
   they were not faithful to his covenant.

4 Yet he who is full of compassion
   forgave their sin and spared them.
   So often he held back his anger
   when he might have stirred up his rage.

SECOND READING   *Philippians 2:6–11*

He humbled himself, therefore God raised him high.

The state of Jesus Christ was divine, yet he did not cling to his equality with God but emptied himself to assume the condition of a slave, and became as men are; and being as all men are, he was humbler yet, even to accepting death, death on a cross. But God raised him high and gave him the name which is above all other names so that all beings in the heavens, on earth and in the underworld, should bend the knee at the name of Jesus and that every tongue should acclaim Jesus Christ as Lord, to the glory of God the Father.

The word of the Lord.
Thanks be to God.

GOSPEL ACCLAMATION

Alleluia, alleluia!
We adore you, O Christ,
and we bless you;
because by your cross
you have redeemed the world.
Alleluia!

GOSPEL   *John 3:13–17*

The Lord be with you.
And with your spirit.

A reading from the holy Gospel according to John.
Glory to you, O Lord.

The Son of Man must be lifted up.

Jesus said to Nicodemus:

'No one has gone up to heaven except the one who came down from heaven, the Son of Man who is in heaven; and the Son of Man must be lifted up as Moses lifted up the serpent in the desert, so that everyone who believes may have eternal life in him. Yes, God loved the world so much that he gave his only Son, so that everyone who believes in him may not be lost but may have eternal life. For God sent his Son into the world not to condemn the world, but so that through him the world might be saved.'

The Gospel of the Lord.
Praise to you, Lord Jesus Christ.

▷ *page 11*

PROFESSION OF FAITH
The Profession of Faith is said when this feast is celebrated on Sunday.

PRAYER OVER THE OFFERINGS
May this oblation, O Lord,
which on the altar of the Cross
cancelled the offence of the whole world,
cleanse us, we pray, of all our sins.
Through Christ our Lord.   **Amen.**

▷ *page 15*

Preface: The victory of the glorious Cross, page 70 or Preface I of the Passion of the Lord, page 71.

COMMUNION ANTIPHON   *John 12:32*
When I am lifted up from the earth,
I will draw everyone to myself, says the Lord.

▷ *page 58*

SAINTS

PRAYER AFTER COMMUNION

Having been nourished by your holy banquet,
we beseech you, Lord Jesus Christ,
to bring those you have redeemed
by the wood of your life-giving Cross
to the glory of the resurrection.
Who live and reign for ever and ever.   **Amen.**

▷ *page 59*

 ALL SAINTS

1 NOVEMBER

If this Solemnity falls on a Sunday, it replaces the Sunday in Ordinary Time.
In certain territories, this Solemnity may be transferred to the nearest Sunday,
replacing the Sunday in Ordinary Time.

ENTRANCE ANTIPHON

Let us all rejoice in the Lord,
as we celebrate the feast day in honour of all the Saints,
at whose festival the Angels rejoice
and praise the Son of God.

▷ *page 7*

COLLECT

Almighty ever-living God,
by whose gift we venerate in one celebration
the merits of all the Saints,
bestow on us, we pray,
through the prayers of so many intercessors,
an abundance of the reconciliation with you
for which we earnestly long.
Through our Lord Jesus Christ, your Son,
who lives and reigns with you in the unity of the Holy Spirit,
one God, for ever and ever.   **Amen.**

FIRST READING   *Apocalypse 7:2–4, 9–14*

I saw a huge number, impossible to count, of people from every nation, race, tribe and language.

I, John, saw another angel rising where the sun rises, carrying the seal of the living God; he called in a powerful voice to the four angels whose duty was to devastate land and sea, 'Wait before you do any damage on land or at sea or to the trees, until we have put the seal on the foreheads of the servants of our God.' Then I heard how many were sealed: a hundred and forty-four thousand, out of all the tribes of Israel.

After that I saw a huge number, impossible to count, of people from every nation, race, tribe and language; they were standing in front of the throne and in front of the Lamb, dressed in white robes and holding palms in their hands. They shouted aloud, 'Victory to our God, who sits on the throne, and to the Lamb!' And all the angels who were standing in a circle round the throne, surrounding the elders and the four animals, prostrated themselves before the throne, and touched the ground with their foreheads, worshipping God with these words, 'Amen. Praise and glory and wisdom and thanksgiving and honour and power and strength to our God for ever and ever. Amen.'

One of the elders then spoke, and asked me, 'Do you know who these people are, dressed in white robes, and where they have come from?' I answered him, 'You can tell me, my Lord.' Then he said, 'These are the people who have been through the great persecution, and they have washed their robes white again in the blood of the Lamb.'

The word of the Lord.
Thanks be to God.

RESPONSORIAL PSALM   *Psalm 23:1–6 response cf v 6*

Such are the men who seek your face, O Lord.

1   The Lord's is the earth and its fullness,
the world and all its peoples.
It is he who set it on the seas;
on the waters he made it firm.

2   Who shall climb the mountain of the Lord?
Who shall stand in his holy place?
The man with clean hands and pure heart,
who desires not worthless things.

3   He shall receive blessings from the Lord
and reward from the God who saves him.
Such are the men who seek him,
seek the face of the God of Jacob.

SECOND READING   *1 John 3:1–3*

We shall see God as he really is.

Think of the love that the Father has lavished on us, by letting us be called God's children; and that is what we are. Because the world refused to acknowledge him, therefore it does not acknowledge us. My dear people, we are already the children of God but what we are to be in the future has not yet been revealed; all we know is, that when it is revealed we shall be like him because we shall see him as he really is. Surely everyone who entertains this hope must purify himself, must try to be as pure as Christ.

The word of the Lord.
Thanks be to God.

GOSPEL ACCLAMATION   *Matthew 11:28*

Alleluia, alleluia!
**Come to me, all you who labour and are overburdened,
and I will give you rest, says the Lord.**
Alleluia!

SAINTS

GOSPEL *Matthew 5:1–12*

The Lord be with you.
And with your spirit.

A reading from the holy Gospel according to Matthew.
Glory to you, O Lord.

Rejoice and be glad, for your reward will be great in heaven.

Seeing the crowds, Jesus went up the hill. There he sat down and was joined by his disciples. Then he began to speak. This is what he taught them:

'How happy are the poor in spirit; theirs is the kingdom of heaven. Happy the gentle: they shall have the earth for their heritage. Happy those who mourn: they shall be comforted. Happy those who hunger and thirst for what is right: they shall be satisfied. Happy the merciful: they shall have mercy shown them. Happy the pure in heart: they shall see God. Happy the peacemakers: they shall be called sons of God. Happy those who are persecuted in the cause of right: theirs is the kingdom of heaven.

'Happy are you when people abuse you and persecute you and speak all kinds of calumny against you on my account. Rejoice and be glad, for your reward will be great in heaven.'

The Gospel of the Lord.
Praise to you, Lord Jesus Christ.

▷ *page 11*

PROFESSION OF FAITH
The Profession of Faith is said.

PRAYER OVER THE OFFERINGS
May these offerings we bring in honour of all the Saints
be pleasing to you, O Lord,
and grant that, just as we believe the Saints
to be already assured of immortality,
so we may experience their concern for our salvation.
Through Christ our Lord.   **Amen.**

▷ *page 15*

Preface: The glory of Jerusalem, our mother, page 71.

COMMUNION ANTIPHON *Matthew 5:8–10*
Blessed are the clean of heart, for they shall see God.
Blessed are the peacemakers,
for they shall be called children of God.
Blessed are they who are persecuted for the sake of righteousness,
for theirs is the Kingdom of Heaven.

▷ *page 58*

PRAYER AFTER COMMUNION

As we adore you, O God, who alone are holy
and wonderful in all your Saints,
we implore your grace,
so that, coming to perfect holiness in the fullness of your love,
we may pass from this pilgrim table
to the banquet of our heavenly homeland.
Through Christ our Lord.   **Amen.**

▷ *page 59*

A solemn blessing may be used.

ALL SOULS' DAY

COMMEMORATION OF ALL THE FAITHFUL DEPARTED (ALL SOULS' DAY)
2 NOVEMBER

*If All Souls' Day falls on a Sunday, it replaces the Sunday in Ordinary Time
unless the Solemnity of All Saints is transferred to Sunday 2 November.
In this case All Souls' Day is transferred to 3 November.*

The celebrant may choose any of the three Masses which follow.

ENTRANCE ANTIPHON

First Mass   *cf 1 Thessalonians 4:14; 1 Corinthians 15:22*

Just as Jesus died and has risen again,
so through Jesus God will bring with him
those who have fallen asleep;
and as in Adam all die,
so also in Christ will all be brought to life.

Second Mass   *cf 4 Esdras 2:34–35*

Eternal rest grant unto them, O Lord,
and let perpetual light shine upon them.

Third Mass   *cf Romans 8:11*

God, who raised Jesus from the dead,
will give life also to your mortal bodies,
through his Spirit that dwells in you.

▷ *page 7*

COLLECT
First Mass
Listen kindly to our prayers, O Lord,
and, as our faith in your Son,
raised from the dead, is deepened,
so may our hope of resurrection for your departed servants
also find new strength.
Through our Lord Jesus Christ, your Son,
who lives and reigns with you in the unity of the Holy Spirit,
one God, for ever and ever.   **Amen.**

Second Mass
O God, glory of the faithful and life of the just,
by the Death and Resurrection of whose Son
we have been redeemed,
look mercifully on your departed servants,
that, just as they professed the mystery of our resurrection,
so they may merit to receive the joys of eternal happiness.
Through our Lord Jesus Christ, your Son,
who lives and reigns with you in the unity of the Holy Spirit,
one God, for ever and ever.   **Amen.**

COLLECT
Third Mass
O God, who willed that your Only Begotten Son,
having conquered death,
should pass over into the realm of heaven,
grant, we pray, to your departed servants
that, with the mortality of this life overcome,
they may gaze eternally on you,
their Creator and Redeemer.
Through our Lord Jesus Christ, your Son,
who lives and reigns with you in the unity of the Holy Spirit,
one God, for ever and ever.   **Amen.**

The following readings are provided in the Lectionary Volume I.
Alternative readings from the Masses for the Dead (Lectionary Volume III) may be chosen.

FIRST READING   *Isaiah 25:6–9*
The Lord will destroy Death for ever.

On this mountain, the Lord of hosts will prepare for all peoples a banquet of rich food. On this mountain, he will remove the mourning veil covering all peoples, and the shroud enwrapping all nations; he will destroy Death for ever. The Lord will wipe away the tears from every cheek; he will take away his people's shame everywhere on earth, for the Lord has said so. That day, it will be said: See, this is our God in whom we hoped for salvation; the Lord is the one in whom we hoped. We exult and we rejoice that he has saved us.

The word of the Lord.
Thanks be to God.

RESPONSORIAL PSALM   *Psalm 26:1, 4, 7–9 13–14 response v 1; alternative response v 13*

The Lord is my light and my help

or

I am sure I shall see the Lord's goodness
in the land of the living.

1   The Lord is my light and my help;
whom shall I hear?
The Lord is the stronghold of my life;
before whom shall I shrink?

2   There is one thing I ask of the Lord,
for this I long,
to live in the house of the Lord,
all the days of my life,
to savour the sweetness of the Lord,
to behold his temple.

3   O Lord, hear my voice when I call;
have mercy and answer.
It is your face, O Lord, that I seek;
hide not your face.

4   I am sure I shall see the Lord's goodness
in the land of the living.
Hope in him, hold firm and take heart.
Hope in the Lord!

SECOND READING   *Romans 5:5–11*

Having died to make us righteous, is it likely that he would now fail to save us from God's anger?

Hope is not deceptive, because the love of God has been poured into our hearts by the Holy Spirit which has been given us. We were still helpless when at his appointed moment Christ died for sinful men. It is not easy to die even for a good man – though of course for someone really worthy, a man might be prepared to die – but what proves that God loves us is that Christ died for us while we were still sinners. Having died to make us righteous, is it likely that he would now fail to save us from God's anger? When we were reconciled to God by the death of his Son, we were still enemies; now that we have been reconciled, surely we may count on being saved by the life of his Son? Not merely because we have been reconciled but because we are filled with joyful trust in God, through our Lord Jesus Christ, through whom we have already gained our reconciliation.

The word of the Lord.
Thanks be to God.

GOSPEL ACCLAMATION   *John 6:39*

Alleluia, alleluia!
It is my Father's will, says the Lord,
that I should lose nothing of all that he has given me,
and that I should raise it up on the last day.
Alleluia!

GOSPEL   *Matthew 11:25–30*

The Lord be with you.
And with your spirit.

A reading from the holy Gospel according to Matthew.
Glory to you, O Lord.

You have hidden these things from the learned and have revealed them to mere children.

Jesus exclaimed: 'I bless you, Father, Lord of heaven and of earth, for hiding these things from the learned and the clever and revealing them to mere children. Yes, Father, for that is what it pleased you to do. Everything has been entrusted to me by my Father; and no one knows the Son except the Father, just as no one knows the Father except the Son and those to whom the Son chooses to reveal him.

'Come to me, all you who labour and are overburdened, and I will give you rest. Shoulder my yoke and learn from me, for I am gentle and humble in heart, and you will find rest for your souls. Yes, my yoke is easy and my burden light.'

The Gospel of the Lord.
Praise to you, Lord Jesus Christ.

▷ *page 11*

PROFESSION OF FAITH
The Profession of Faith is said when this commemoration is celebrated on Sunday.

PRAYER OVER THE OFFERINGS
First Mass
Look favourably on our offerings, O Lord,
so that your departed servants
may be taken up into glory with your Son,
in whose great mystery of love we are all united.
Who lives and reigns for ever and ever. **Amen.**

Second Mass
Almighty and merciful God,
by means of these sacrificial offerings
wash away, we pray, in the Blood of Christ,
the sins of your departed servants,
for you purify unceasingly by your merciful forgiveness
those you once cleansed in the waters of Baptism.
Through Christ our Lord. **Amen.**

Third Mass

Receive, Lord, in your kindness,
the sacrificial offering we make
for all your servants who sleep in Christ,
that, set free from the bonds of death
by this singular sacrifice,
they may merit eternal life.
Through Christ our Lord.   **Amen.**

▷ *page 15*

Preface for the Dead I–V, pages 71–72.

COMMUNION ANTIPHON

First Mass   *cf John 11:25–26*

I am the Resurrection and the Life, says the Lord.
Whoever believes in me, even though he dies, will live,
and everyone who lives and believes in me will not die for ever.

Second Mass   *cf 4 Esdras 2:35, 34*

Let perpetual light shine upon them, O Lord,
with your Saints for ever, for you are merciful.

Third Mass   *cf Philippians 3:20–21*

We await a saviour, the Lord Jesus Christ,
who will change our mortal bodies,
to conform with his glorified body.

▷ *page 58*

PRAYER AFTER COMMUNION

First Mass

Grant we pray, O Lord, that your departed servants,
for whom we have celebrated this paschal Sacrament,
may pass over to a dwelling place of light and peace.
Through Christ our Lord.   **Amen.**

Second Mass

Having received the Sacrament of your Only Begotten Son,
who was sacrificed for us and rose in glory,
we humbly implore you, O Lord,
for your departed servants,
that, cleansed by the paschal mysteries,
they may glory in the gift of the resurrection to come.
Through Christ our Lord.   **Amen.**

Third Mass

Through these sacrificial gifts
which we have received, O Lord,
bestow on your departed servants your great mercy
and, to those you have endowed with the grace of Baptism,
grant also the fullness of eternal joy.
Through Christ our Lord.   **Amen.**

▷ *page 59*

A solemn blessing may be used.

DEDICATION OF THE LATERAN BASILICA

9 NOVEMBER
If this feast falls on a Sunday, it replaces the Sunday in Ordinary Time.
When the Feast is celebrated on a weekday there is only one reading before the Gospel.

ENTRANCE ANTIPHON   *cf Revelation 21:2*

I saw the holy city, a new Jerusalem,
coming down out of heaven from God,
prepared like a bride adorned for her husband.

or   *cf Revelation 21:3*

Behold God's dwelling with the human race.
He will dwell with them and they will be his people,
and God himself with them will be their God.

▷ *page 7*

COLLECT

O God, who from living and chosen stones
prepare an eternal dwelling for your majesty,
increase in your Church the spirit of grace you have bestowed,
so that by new growth your faithful people
may build up the heavenly Jerusalem.
Through our Lord Jesus Christ, your Son,
who lives and reigns with you in the unity of the Holy Spirit,
one God, for ever and ever. **Amen.**

or

O God, who were pleased to call your Church the Bride,
grant that the people that serves your name
may revere you, love you and follow you,
and may be led by you
to attain your promises in heaven.
Through our Lord Jesus Christ, your Son,
who lives and reigns with you in the unity of the Holy Spirit,
one God, for ever and ever. **Amen.**

FIRST READING   *Ezekiel 47:1–2, 8–9, 12*

I saw a stream of water coming from the Temple, bringing life to all wherever it flowed.

The angel brought me to the entrance of the Temple, where a stream came out from under the Temple threshold and flowed eastwards, since the Temple faced east. The water flowed from under the right side of the Temple, south of the altar. He took me out by the north gate and led me right round outside as far as the outer east gate where the water flowed out on the right-hand side. The man went to the east holding his measuring line and measured off a thousand cubits; he then made me wade across the stream; the water reached my ankles. He measured off another thousand and made me wade across the stream again; the water reached my knees. He measured off another thousand and made me wade across again; the water reached my waist. He measured off another thousand; it was now a river which I could not cross;

the stream had swollen and was now deep water, a river impossible to cross. He then said: 'Do you see, son of man?' He took me further, then brought me back to the bank of the river. When I got back, there were many trees on each bank of the river. He said, 'This water flows east down to the Arabah and to the sea; and flowing into the sea it makes its waters wholesome. Wherever the river flows, all living creatures teeming in it will live. Fish will be very plentiful, for wherever the water goes it brings health, and life teems wherever the river flows. Along the river, on either bank, will grow every kind of fruit tree with leaves that never wither and fruit that never fails; they will bear new fruit every month, because this water comes from the sanctuary. And their fruit will be good to eat and the leaves medicinal.'

The word of the Lord.

Thanks be to God.

RESPONSORIAL PSALM   *Psalm 45:2–3, 5–6 8–9 response v 5*

**The waters of a river give joy to God's city,
the holy place where the Most High dwells.**

1   God is for us a refuge and strength,
    a helper close at hand, in time of distress;
    so we shall not fear though the earth should rock,
    though the mountains fall into the depths of the sea.

2   The waters of a river give joy to God's city,
    the holy place where the Most High dwells.
    God is within, it cannot be shaken;
    God will help it at the dawning of the day.

3   The Lord of hosts is with us:
    the God of Jacob is our stronghold.
    Come, consider the works of the Lord,
    the redoubtable deeds he has done on the earth.

SECOND READING   *1 Corinthians 3:9–11, 16–17*

You are the temple of God.

You are God's building. By the grace God gave me, I succeeded as an architect and laid the foundations, on which someone else is doing the building. Everyone doing the building must work carefully. For the foundation, nobody can lay any other than the one which has already been laid, that is Jesus Christ. Didn't you realise that you were God's temple and that the Spirit of God was living among you? If anybody should destroy the temple of God, God will destroy him, because the temple of God is sacred; and you are that temple.

The word of the Lord.

Thanks be to God.

GOSPEL ACCLAMATION   *2 Chronicles 7:16*

**Alleluia, alleluia!
I have chosen and consecrated this house, says the Lord,
for my name to be there for ever.
Alleluia!**

GOSPEL   *John 2:13–22*

The Lord be with you.
And with your spirit.

A reading from the holy Gospel according to John.
Glory to you, O Lord.

He was speaking of the sanctuary that was his body.

Just before the Jewish Passover Jesus went up to Jerusalem, and in the Temple he found people selling cattle and sheep and pigeons, and the money changers sitting at their counters there. Making a whip out of some cord, he drove them all out of the Temple, cattle and sheep as well, scattered the money changers' coins, knocked their tables over and said to the pigeon-sellers, 'Take all this out of here and stop turning my Father's house into a market.' Then his disciples remembered the words of scripture: Zeal for your house will devour me. The Jews intervened and said, 'What sign can you show us to justify what you have done?' Jesus answered, 'Destroy this sanctuary, and in three days I will raise it up.' The Jews replied, 'It has taken forty-six years to build this sanctuary: are you going to raise it up in three days?' But he was speaking of the sanctuary that was his body, and when Jesus rose from the dead, his disciples remembered that he had said this, and they believed the scripture and the words he had said.

The Gospel of the Lord.
Praise to you, Lord Jesus Christ.

▷ page 11

PROFESSION OF FAITH

The Profession of Faith is said when this feast is celebrated on Sunday.

PRAYER OVER THE OFFERINGS

Accept, we pray, O Lord, the offering made here
and grant that by it those who seek your favour
may receive in this place
the power of the Sacraments
and the answer to their prayers.
Through Christ our Lord.   **Amen.**

▷ page 15

Preface: The Mystery of the Church, the Bride of Christ and the Temple of the Spirit, page 73.

COMMUNION ANTIPHON   *cf 1 Peter 2:5*

Be built up like living stones,
into a spiritual house, a holy priesthood.

▷ page 58

PRAYER AFTER COMMUNION

O God, who chose to foreshadow for us
the heavenly Jerusalem
through the sign of your Church on earth,
grant, we pray,
that, by our partaking of this Sacrament,
we may be made the temple of your grace
and may enter the dwelling place of your glory.
Through Christ our Lord.   **Amen.**

▷ page 59

A solemn blessing may be used.

OTHER CELEBRATIONS

ANNIVERSARY OF DEDICATION OF A CHURCH

COMMON OF THE DEDICATION OF A CHURCH
ON THE ANNIVERSARY OF THE DEDICATION
I IN THE CHURCH THAT WAS DEDICATED

ENTRANCE ANTIPHON   *Psalm 67:36*

Wonderful are you, O God in your holy place.
The God of Israel himself gives his people strength and courage.
Blessed be God!

▷ *page 7*

The Gloria is sung (or said).

COLLECT
O God, who year by year renew for us the day
when this your holy temple was consecrated,
hear the prayers of your people
and grant that in this place
for you there may always be pure worship
and for us, fullness of redemption.
Through our Lord Jesus Christ, your Son,
who lives and reigns with you in the unity of the Holy Spirit,
one God, for ever and ever.   **Amen.**

FIRST READING

*The Lectionary notes that the pairings of Readings with Responsorial Psalms are suggestions only.
Any other suitable pairing may be used, having regard to the pastoral needs of the occasion.*

One of the following readings is chosen:

1   1 Kings 8:22–23, 27–30
    Let your eyes watch over this house.

2   2 Chronicles 5:6–11, 13–6:2
    *I have built you a dwelling, a place
    for you to live in for ever.*

3   Isaiah 56:1, 6–7
    My house will be called a house of prayer for all the peoples.

4   Ezekiel 43:1–2, 4–7
    I saw the glory of the Lord fill the Temple.

5   Ezekiel 47:1–2, 8–9, 12
    I saw a stream of water coming from the Temple, bringing life to all wherever it flowed.

RESPONSORIAL PSALM

One of the following Psalms is chosen:

FOR READING 5,

PSALM 45   *Psalm 45:2–3, 5–6, 8–9 response v 5*

> The waters of a river give joy to God's city,
> the holy place where the Most High dwells.

FOR READING 1 OR 3

PSALM 83   *Psalm 83:3–5, 10–11 response v 2, alternative response Apocalypse 21:3*

> How lovely is your dwelling place,
> Lord, God of hosts

or

> Here God lives among men.

FOR READING 2 OR 4

1 CHRONICLES 29   *1 Chronicles 29:10–12 response v 13*

> We praise your glorious name, O Lord.

SECOND READING

One of the following readings is chosen:

1   1 Corinthians 3:9–11, 16–17

> *You are the temple of God.*

2   Ephesians 2:19–22

> *All grow into one holy temple in the Lord.*

3   Hebrews 12:18–19, 22–24

> *You have come to Mount Zion and to the city of the living God.*

4   1 Peter 2:4–9

> *So that you too may be living stones making a spiritual house.*

GOSPEL ACCLAMATION

The Lectionary notes that the pairings of each Gospel Acclamations with Gospel readings are suggestions only. Any other suitable pairing may be used, having regard to the pastoral needs of the occasion.

FOR GOSPEL 1   *Matthew 16:18*

> Alleluia, alleluia!
> You are Peter and on this rock I will build my Church.
> And the gates of the underworld can never hold out against it.
> Alleluia!

FOR GOSPEL 2   *cf Matthew 7:8*

> Alleluia, alleluia!
> In my house, says the Lord,
> the one who asks always receives;
> the one who searches always finds;
> the one who knocks will always have the door opened to him.
> Alleluia!

FOR GOSPEL 3   *2 Chronicles 7:16*

> Alleluia, alleluia!
> I have chosen and consecrated this house, says the Lord,
> that my name may remain in it for all time.
> Alleluia!

FOR GOSPEL 4   *Isaiah 66:1*

> **Alleluia, alleluia!**
> **With heaven my throne**
> **and earth my footstool,**
> **what house could you build me? says the Lord.**
> **Alleluia!**

or   *Ezekiel 37:27*

> **Alleluia, alleluia!**
> **I shall make my home among them, says the Lord;**
> **I will be their God,**
> **they shall be my people**
> **Alleluia!**

GOSPEL

One of the following readings is chosen:

1   Matthew 16:13–19

> *You are Peter. I will give you the keys*
> *of the kingdom of heaven.*

2   Luke 19:1–10

> *Today salvation has come to this house.*

3   John 2:13–22

> *He was speaking of the sanctuary*
> *that was his body.*

4   John 4:19–24

> *True worshippers will worship the Father*
> *in spirit and truth.*

▷ *page 11*

The Profession of Faith is said.

PRAYER OVER THE OFFERINGS

Recalling the day when you were pleased
to fill your house with glory and holiness, O Lord,
we pray that you may make of us
a sacrificial offering always acceptable to you.
Through Christ our Lord.   **Amen.**

▷ *page 15*

PREFACE

THE MYSTERY OF THE TEMPLE OF GOD, WHICH IS THE CHURCH.

Priest: The Lord be with you.
People: **And with your spirit.**

Priest: Lift up your hearts.
People: **We lift them up to the Lord.**

Priest: Let us give thanks to the Lord our God.
People: **It is right and just.**

Priest: It is truly right and just, our duty and our salvation,
always and everywhere to give you thanks,
Lord, holy Father, almighty and eternal God,
through Christ our Lord.

For in this visible house that you have let us build
and where you never cease to show favour

to the family on pilgrimage to you in this place,
you wonderfully manifest and accomplish
the mystery of your communion with us.
Here you build up for yourself the temple that we are
and cause your Church, spread throughout the world,
to grow ever more and more as the Lord's own Body,
till she reaches her fullness in the vision of peace,
the heavenly city of Jerusalem.

And so, with the countless ranks of the blessed,
in the temple of your glory we praise you,
we bless you, and proclaim your greatness, as we acclaim:

All: **Holy, Holy, Holy Lord God of hosts...**

COMMUNION ANTIPHON   *cf 1 Corinthians 3:16–17*

You are the temple of God, and the Spirit of God dwells in you.
The temple of God, which you are, is holy.

▷ *page 58*

PRAYER AFTER COMMUNION

May the people consecrated to you, O Lord, we pray,
receive the fruits and joy of your blessing,
that the festive homage
they have offered you today in the body
may redound upon them as a spiritual gift.
Through Christ our Lord.   **Amen.**

▷ *page 59*

BLESSING AT THE END OF MASS

Priest: May God, the Lord of heaven and earth,
who has gathered you today
in memory of the dedication of this church,
make you abound in heavenly blessings.
All: **Amen.**

Priest: And may he, who has willed that all his scattered children
be gathered together in his Son,
grant that you may become his temple
and the dwelling place of the Holy Spirit.
All: **Amen.**

Priest: Thus, may you be made thoroughly clean,
so that God may dwell within you
and you may possess with all the Saints
the inheritance of eternal happiness.
All: **Amen.**

Priest: And may the blessing of almighty God,
the Father, and the Son, ✠ and the Holy Spirit,
come down on you and remain with you for ever.
All: **Amen.**

RCIA — RITE OF ACCEPTANCE

RITE OF CHRISTIAN INITIATION OF ADULTS
RITE OF ACCEPTANCE INTO THE ORDER OF CATECHUMENS

The Introductory Rites of the Mass are replaced by the act of Receiving the Candidates.

RECEIVING THE CANDIDATES

The candidates, their sponsors and a group of the faithful gather outside the church or at the church door (or elsewhere suitable to this rite).

The assembly may sing a Psalm or appropriate song.

GREETING

The Priest greets the candidates in a friendly manner. He speaks to them, their sponsors and all present about their journey of faith to this point.

He invites the sponsors and candidates to come forward.
As they take their places before the Priest, an appropriate song may be sung
(for example Psalm 62:1–8).

OPENING DIALOGUE

The candidates may be introduced to the assembly, or their names called out. The Priest then asks the candidates their intentions.

In asking the candidates about their intentions celebrant may use other words than those provided the and may let them answer in their own words for example, to the first question,

'What do you ask of the Church of God?' or 'What do you desire?' or 'For what reason have you come?',

he may receive such answers as 'The grace of Christ' or 'Entrance into the Church' or 'Eternal life' or other suitable responses. The celebrant then phrases his next question according to the answer received.

Priest:	What do you ask of God's Church?
Candidate:	**Faith.**

Priest:	What does faith offer you?
Candidate:	**Eternal life.**

CANDIDATES' FIRST ACCEPTANCE OF THE GOSPEL

The Priest addresses the candidates and then asks them about their acceptance of the Gospel. His question may end in these or similar words:

Priest:	…Are you prepared to begin this journey under the guidance of Christ?
Candidates:	**I am.**

AFFIRMATION BY THE SPONSORS AND THE ASSEMBLY

The Priest then asks the sponsors and the assembly to commit themselves to support the candidates. He uses these or similar words:

Priest: Sponsors, you now present these candidates to us; are you, and all who are gathered here with us, ready to help these candidates find and follow Christ?

All: **We are.**

Then the Priest says:

Priest: Father of mercy,
            we thank you for these your servants.
            You have sought and summoned them in many ways
            and they have turned to seek you.

            You have called them today
            and they have answered in your presence:
            we praise you, Lord, and we bless you.

All sing or say:

All: **We praise you, Lord, and we bless you.**

SIGNING OF THE CANDIDATES WITH THE CROSS

The catechists or sponsors sign the catechumens on the forehead as the Priest says:

Priest: N., receive the cross on your forehead.
            It is Christ himself who now strengthens you
            with this sign of his love.
            Learn to know him and follow him.

All say or sing this, or another suitable acclamation:

All: **Glory and praise to you, Lord Jesus Christ!**

Other parts of the body may also be signed with the Sign of the Cross. The catechists or sponsors sign the catechumens on the appropriate part of the body as the Priest says each set of words.

Priest: Receive the sign of the cross on your ears,
            that you may hear the voice of the Lord.

All: **Glory and praise to you, Lord Jesus Christ!**

Priest: Receive the sign of the cross on your eyes,
            that you may see the glory of the Lord.

All: **Glory and praise to you, Lord Jesus Christ!**

Priest: Receive the sign of the cross on your lips,
            that you may respond to the word of God.

All: **Glory and praise to you, Lord Jesus Christ!**

Priest: Receive the sign of the cross on your heart,
            that Christ may dwell there by faith.

All: **Glory and praise to you, Lord Jesus Christ!**

Priest: Receive the sign of the cross on your shoulders,
that you may bear the gentle yoke of Christ.

All: **Glory and praise to you, Lord Jesus Christ!**

Then the celebrant alone makes the sign of the cross over all the candidates at once:

Priest: I sign you with the sign of eternal life
in the name of the Father, and of the Son ✠
and of the Holy Spirit.

Catechumens: **Amen.**

CONCLUDING PRAYER

Let us pray.

Lord,
we have signed these catechumens
with the sign of Christ's cross.
Protect them by its power,
so that, faithful to the grace which has
    begun in them,
they may keep your commandments
and come to the glory of rebirth in baptism.

We ask this through Christ our Lord.

Amen.

or

Almighty God,
by the cross and resurrection of your Son
you have given life to your people.
Your servants have received the sign of
    the cross:
make them living proof of its saving power
and help them to persevere in the footsteps
    of Christ.

We ask this through Christ our Lord.

Amen.

INVITATION TO THE CELEBRATION OF THE WORD OF GOD

The Priest invites the catechumens and their sponsors to enter the church, using these or similar words:

Priest: N. and N., come into the church,
to share with us at the table of God's word.

The catechumens and their sponsors enter the church to take their places among the assembly.

*During the entry an appropriate song is sung, or the following antiphon may be used
with Psalm 33:2, 3, 6, 9, 10, 11,16.*

Ant.   Come, my children, and listen to me;
I will teach you the fear of the Lord.

LITURGY OF THE WORD

INSTRUCTION

*After the catechumens have taken their places among the assembly, the Priest speaks to them helping them
understand the dignity of God's word which is proclaimed and heard in the church.*

The Lectionary is carried in procession and placed with honour on the ambo, where it may be incensed.

READINGS

*The readings may be chosen from any of the readings of the Lectionary for Mass that are suited to the new
catechumens.*

HOMILY

A homily follows that explains the readings.

PRESENTATION OF A BIBLE *(Optional)*

A book containing the gospels may be given to the catechumens by the celebrant; a cross may also be given, unless this has already been done as one of the additional rites.

INTERCESSIONS FOR THE CATECHUMENS

Each intercession for the catechumens concludes:

Let us pray to the Lord
Lord, hear our prayer

If the Prayer of the Faithful is to be omitted, intercessions for the Church and the whole world are added to the intercessions for the catechumens.

PRAYER OVER THE CATECHUMENS

After the intercessions, the celebrant, with hands outstretched over the catechumens, says one of the following prayers.

Let us pray.
[God of our forebears and] God of all creation,
we ask you to look favourably on your servants *N.* and *N.;*
make them fervent in spirit,
joyful in hope,
and always ready to serve your name.
Lead them, Lord, to the baptism of new birth,
so that, living a fruitful life in the company of your faithful,
they may receive the eternal reward that you promise.
We ask this in the name of Jesus the Lord. **Amen.**

or

Almighty God,
source of all creation,
you have made us in your image.
Welcome with love those who come before you today.
They have listened among us to the word of Christ;
by its power renew them
and by your grace refashion them,
so that in time they may assume the full likeness of Christ,
who lives and reigns for ever and ever.   **Amen.**

DISMISSAL OF THE CATECHUMENS

If the eucharist is to be celebrated, the catechumens are normally dismissed at this point by use of option A; if the catechumens are to stay for the celebration of the eucharist, option B is used; if the eucharist is not to be celebrated, the entire assembly is dismissed by use of option C.

A   *The celebrant recalls briefly the great joy with which the catechumens have just been received and urges them to live according to the word of God they have just heard. After the dismissal formulary, the group of catechumens goes out but does not disperse. With the help of some of the faithful, the catechumens remain together to share their joy and spiritual experiences.*

Priest: Catechumens, go in peace,
                 and may the Lord remain with you always.
Catechumens: **Thanks be to God.**

Similar words may be used, for example:
Priest: My dear friends,
          this community now sends you forth
          to reflect more deeply on the word of God which you have shared with us today.
          Be assured of our loving support and prayers for you.
          We look forward to the day when you will share fully in the Lord's Table.

B   *If for serious reasons the catechumens cannot leave and must remain with the baptized, they are to be instructed that though they are present at the eucharist, they cannot take part in it as the baptized do. They may be reminded of this by the celebrant in these or similar words.*

Priest: Although you cannot yet participate fully in the Lord's eucharist,
          stay with us as a sign of our hope
          that all God's children will eat and drink with the Lord
          and work with his Spirit to re-create the face of the earth.

C   *The celebrant dismisses those present, using these or similar words.*

Priest: Go in peace, and may the Lord remain with you always.
All: **Thanks be to God.**

An appropriate song may conclude the celebration.

▷ *page 13*

PRAYER OF THE FAITHFUL AND PROFESSION OF FAITH

Intercessory prayer is resumed with the usual Prayer of the Faithful for the needs of the Church and the whole world; then, if required, the Profession of Faith is said. But for pastoral reasons, the Prayer of the Faithful and the Profession of Faith may be omitted.

Mass continues in the usual way, using the prayers proper to the day.

After the celebration of the Rite of Acceptance, the names of the catechumens are to be duly inscribed in the register of catechumens, along with the names of the sponsors and the minister and the date and place of the celebration...

...Joined to the Church, the catechumens are now part of the household of Christ, since the Church nourishes them with the word of God and by means of liturgical celebrations.

cf Rite of Christian Initiation of Adults n 46–47

MUSIC FOR THE ORDER OF MASS

On occasion, music is not provided for the text which precedes the people's response. In this case a cue is given indicating the last note(s) sung before the response, as in the example opposite:

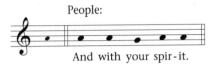

People:

And with your spir-it.

INTRODUCTORY RITES

SIGN OF THE CROSS

All make the Sign of the Cross as the Priest sings:

Priest:

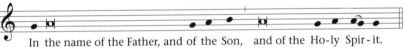

In the name of the Father, and of the Son, and of the Ho-ly Spir-it.

People:

A-men.

MUSIC

GREETING

Priest: The grace of our Lord Jesus Christ,
          and the love of God,
          and the communion of the Holy Spirit
          be with you all.

or

Priest: Grace to you and peace from God our Father
          and the Lord Jesus Christ.

or

Priest: The Lord be with you.

A Bishop will say:

Bishop: Peace be with you.

People:

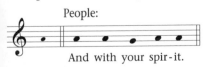

And with your spir-it.

PENITENTIAL ACT
Penitential Act B

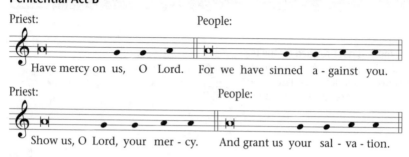

Penitential Act C

Priest or minister: You were sent to heal the contrite of heart:

Repeat after the Priest or minister:

Priest or minister: You came to call sinners:

Repeat after the Priest or minister:

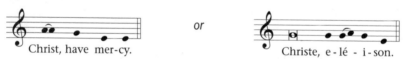

Priest or minister: You are seated at the right hand of the Father
                 to intercede for us:

Repeat after the Priest or minister:

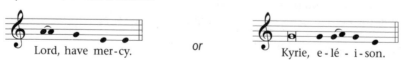

ABSOLUTION

The absolution by the Priest follows all of the options above

Priest:

May almighty God have mercy on us, forgive us our sins,

People:

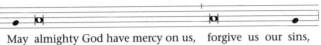

and bring us to ever-last-ing life.   A-men.

KYRIE

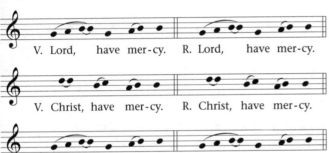

V. Lord,   have mer-cy.   R. Lord,   have mer-cy.

V. Christ, have mer-cy.   R. Christ, have mer-cy.

V. Lord,   have mer-cy.   R. Lord,   have mer-cy.

or

V. Ky-ri - e,   e - lé - i-son.   R. Ky-ri - e, e - lé - i-son.

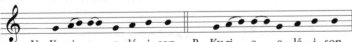

V. Chri - ste, e - lé - i-son.   R. Chri-ste,   e - lé - i-son.

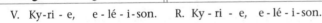

V. Ky-ri - e,   e - lé - i-son.   R. Ky-ri - e, e - lé - i-son.

or

R. Ky - ri - e,   e - lé - i - son.

GLORIA

Glo-ry to God in the high-est, and on earth peace to peo-ple of good will.

We praise you, we bless you, we a-dore you, we glo-ri-fy you,

we give you thanks for your great glo-ry, Lord God, heav-en-ly King,

O God, al-migh-ty Fa-ther. Lord Je-sus Christ,

On-ly Be-got-ten Son, Lord, God, Lamb of God, Son of the Fa-ther,

you take a-way the sins of the world, have mer-cy on us;

you take a-way the sins of the world, re-ceive our prayer;

you are seat-ed at the right hand of the Fa-ther, have mer-cy on us.

For you a-lone are the Ho-ly One, you a-lone are the Lord,

you a-lone are the Most High, Je-sus Christ, with the Ho-ly Spir-it,

in the glo-ry of God the Fa - ther. A - men.

FIRST READING

Acclamation at the end of the reading.

Reader: People:

The word of the Lord. Thanks be to God.

SECOND READING

Acclamation at the end of the reading.

Reader: People:

The word of the Lord. Thanks be to God.

GOSPEL

Dialogue at the beginning of the Gospel.

Deacon / Priest: People:

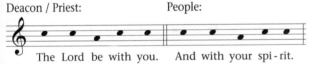

The Lord be with you. And with your spi-rit.

Deacon / Priest: People:

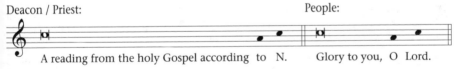

A reading from the holy Gospel according to N. Glory to you, O Lord.

Acclamation at the end of the Gospel.

Deacon / Priest: People:

The Gospel of the Lord. Praise to you, Lord Je-sus Christ.

MUSIC

PROFESSION OF FAITH

Niceno-Constantinopolitan Creed

I be-lieve in one God, the Fa-ther al-migh-ty, mak-er of heav-en

and earth, of all things vis - i - ble and in - vis - i - ble.

I be-lieve in one Lord Je-sus Christ, the Only Be - got-ten Son of God,

born of the Father be - fore all a - ges. God from God, Light from Light,

true God from true God, be - got-ten, not made, con-sub-stan-tial

with the Fa-ther; through him all things were made. For us men and for

At the words that follow, up to and

our sal - va-tion he came down from heav-en, and by the Ho-ly Spir-it

including 'and became man', all bow.

was in - car-nate of the Vir-gin Mar - y, and be-came man.

For our sake he was cru - ci - fied un - der Pon - tius Pi - late,

he suffered death and was bur - ied, and rose a-gain on the third day

LITURGY OF THE EUCHARIST

ORATE, FRATRES

ALL STAND

Priest:

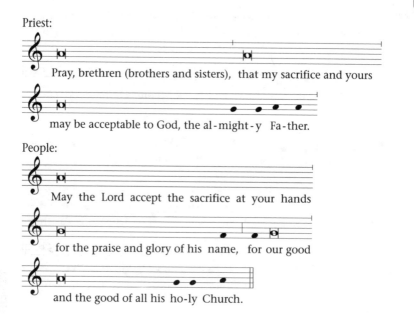

Pray, brethren (brothers and sisters), that my sacrifice and yours

may be acceptable to God, the al-might-y Fa-ther.

People:

May the Lord accept the sacrifice at your hands

for the praise and glory of his name, for our good

and the good of all his ho-ly Church.

PREFACE DIALOGUE

Priest: All:

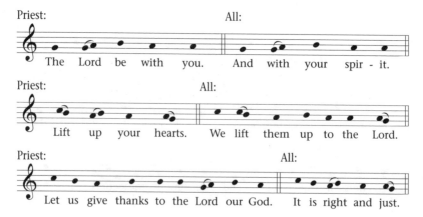

The Lord be with you. And with your spir-it.

Priest: All:

Lift up your hearts. We lift them up to the Lord.

Priest: All:

Let us give thanks to the Lord our God. It is right and just.

SANCTUS

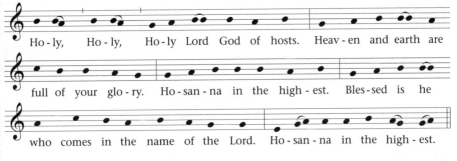

Ho-ly, Ho-ly, Ho-ly Lord God of hosts. Heav-en and earth are full of your glo-ry. Ho-san-na in the high-est. Bles-sed is he who comes in the name of the Lord. Ho-san-na in the high-est.

or

San-ctus, San-ctus, San-ctus Dó-mi-nus De-us Sá-ba-oth. Ple-ni sunt cae-li et ter-ra gló-ri-a tu-a. Ho-sán-na in ex-cél-sis. Be-ne-dí-ctus qui ven-it in nó-mi-ne Dó-mi-ni. Ho-sán-na in ex-cél-sis.

MEMORIAL ACCLAMATION

Priest:

The mys-ter-y of faith.

Memorial Acclamation A

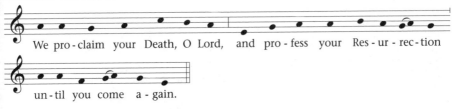

We pro-claim your Death, O Lord, and pro-fess your Res-ur-rec-tion un-til you come a-gain.

Priest:

The mys - ter - y of faith.

Memorial Acclamation B

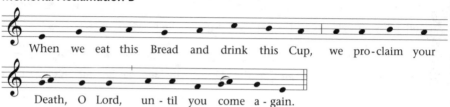

When we eat this Bread and drink this Cup, we pro-claim your

Death, O Lord, un - til you come a - gain.

Memorial Acclamation C

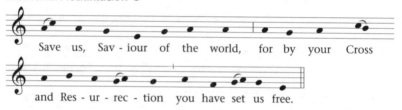

Save us, Sav - iour of the world, for by your Cross

and Res - ur - rec - tion you have set us free.

Memorial Acclamation D   *for Ireland only*

My Lord and my God.

DOXOLOGY AND GREAT AMEN

Priest:

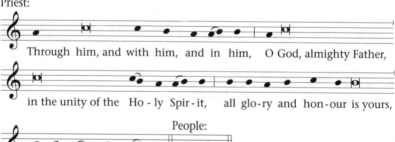

Through him, and with him, and in him, O God, almighty Father,

in the unity of the Ho - ly Spir - it, all glo-ry and hon-our is yours,

People:

for ev - er and ev - er. A - men.

COMMUNION RITE

LORD'S PRAYER

Our Fa-ther, who art in heav-en, hal-lowed be thy name;

thy king-dom come, thy will be done on earth as it is in heav-en.

Give us this day our dai-ly bread, and for-give us our tres-pass-es,

as we for-give those who tres-pass a-gainst us; and lead us not

in-to temp-ta-tion, but de-liv-er us from e-vil.

Priest   Deliver us, Lord, we pray, from every evil,
          graciously grant peace in our days,
          that, by the help of your mercy,
          we may be always free from sin
          and safe from all distress,
          as we await the blessed hope
          and the coming of our Saviour, Jesus Christ.

People:

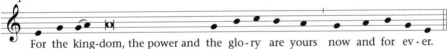

For the king-dom, the power and the glo-ry are yours now and for ev-er.

RITE OF PEACE

Priest: The peace of the Lord be with you always.

People:

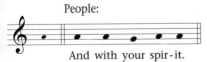

And with your spir-it.

BREAKING OF BREAD

Lamb of God, you take a-way the sins of the world, have mer-cy on us.

Lamb of God, you take a-way the sins of the world, have mer-cy on us.

Lamb of God, you take a-way the sins of the world, grant us peace.

or

Ag - nus De - i, qui tol-lis pec-cá-ta mun-di: mi-se - ré - re no-bis.

Ag - nus De - i, qui tol-lis pec-cá-ta mun-di: mi-se - ré - re no-bis.

Ag - nus De - i, qui tol-lis pec-cá-ta mun-di: do-na no-bis pa-cem.

The invocation may be repeated several times if the Breaking of the Bread is prolonged.
The final time always ends 'grant us peace' ('dona nobis pacem').

INVITATION TO COMMUNION

Priest   Behold the Lamb of God,
           behold him who takes away the sins of the world.
           Blessed are those called to the...

People:

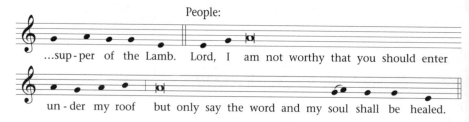

...sup-per of the Lamb. Lord, I am not worthy that you should enter

un - der my roof but only say the word and my soul shall be healed.

BLESSING

Priest: People:

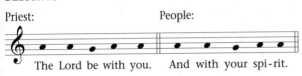

The Lord be with you.   And with your spi-rit.

On certain occasions, the following blessing may be preceded by a solemn blessing or prayer over the people. Then the Priest blesses the people, singing:

Priest: May almighty God bless you:
            the Father, and the Son, ✠ and the Holy Spirit.

Priest: People:

...Ho-ly Spi - rit.   A - men.

In a Pontifical Mass, the celebrant receives the mitre and sings:

Bishop: All:

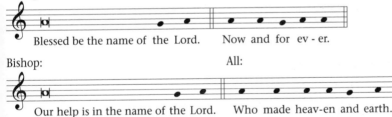

Blessed be the name of the Lord.   Now and for ev - er.

Bishop: All:

Our help is in the name of the Lord.   Who made heav-en and earth.

On certain occasions the following blessing may be preceded by a more solemn blessing or prayer over the people. Then the celebrant receives the pastoral staff, if he uses it, and sings:

Bishop: May almighty God bless you:
making the Sign of the Cross over the people three times, he adds:
            the Father, ✠ and the Son, ✠ and the...

Bishop: People:

...Ho-ly Spi - rit.   A - men.

If any liturgical action follows immediately, the rites of dismissal are omitted.

MUSIC

DISMISSAL

Deacon or Priest: Go forth, the Mass is ended.
or   Go and announce the Gospel of the Lord.
or   Go in peace, glorifying the Lord by your life.

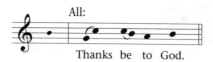

Thanks be to God.

or

Go in peace.   Thanks be to God.

THOUGHTS AND PRAYERS

Prayer Before a Crucifix

Behold, O kind and most sweet Jesus,
I cast myself on my knees in your sight,
and with the most fervent desire of my soul,
I pray and beseech you
that you would impress upon my heart
lively sentiments of faith, hope and charity,
with a true repentance for my sins
and a firm desire of amendment,
while with deep affection and grief of soul

I ponder within myself
and mentally contemplate
your five most precious wounds,
having before my eyes
that which David spoke in prophecy of you,
O good Jesus:
'They have pierced my hands and my feet;
they have numbered all my bones.'

On Silence

We need to find God, and he cannot be found in noise and restlessness,
God is the friend of silence.
See how nature – trees, flowers, grass – grow in silence;
see the stars, the moon and sun, how they move in silence.
Is not our mission to give God to the poor in the slums?
Not a dead God, but a living, loving God.
The more we receive in silent prayer, the more we can give in our active life.
We need silence to be able to touch souls.
The essential thing is not what we say, but what God says to us and through us.
All our words will be useless unless they come from within –
words which do not give the light of Christ increase the darkness.

Mother Teresa

Prayers to Mary

The Memorare

Remember, O most loving Virgin Mary,
that it is a thing unheard of,
that anyone ever had recourse to your
protection,
implored your help,
or sought your intercession,
and was left forsaken.
Filled therefore with confidence in your
goodness
I fly to you, O Mother, Virgin of virgins.
To you I come, before you I stand,
a sorrowful sinner.
Despise not my poor words,
O Mother of the Word of God,
but graciously hear and grant my prayer.

Hail, Holy Queen

Hail, holy Queen, mother of mercy:
hail, our life, our sweetness, and our hope!
To you do we cry,
poor banished children of Eve.
To you do we send up our sighs,
mourning and weeping
in this vale of tears.
Turn then, most gracious advocate,
your eyes of mercy towards us;
and after this our exile,
show to us
the blessed fruit of your womb, Jesus.
O clement,
O loving,
O sweet Virgin Mary.
Pray for us, O holy Mother of God.
That we may be made worthy
    of the promises of Christ.

Anima Christi

Soul of Christ, sanctify me.
Body of Christ, save me.
Blood of Christ, inebriate me.
Water from the side of Christ, wash me.
Passion of Christ, strengthen me.

Jesus, hear me.
Hide me in your wounds,
that I may never leave your side
and never let me be parted from you.
From the malicious enemy defend me.

In the hour of my death call me,
and tell me come unto you,
that with your saints I may praise you
through all eternity,
for ever and ever. Amen

O Sacrum Convivium

O Sacred Banquet,
in which Christ is received,
and the memory of his Passion is renewed;
where the soul is filled with grace,
and a pledge of future glory is given to us.

PRAYERS AFTER MASS

Prayer of Saint Ignatius

Teach us, good Lord,
to serve you as you deserve;
to give and not to count the cost;
to fight and not to heed the wounds;
to toil, and not to seek for rest;
to labour and to ask for no reward,
save that of knowing
that we do your will;
through Jesus Christ our Lord.

Jesus, Our Brother

Dear Lord,
I believe that Holy Communion joins us all
together in union with you and in union
with one another.

As we all received you together at the
Holy Table, let us remember that we are all
members of one family.

Let us help one another and forgive one
another, bearing one another's burdens.

You have said that if we do not love our
neighbour, whom we can see, how can we
love God, whom we cannot see?

Make me careful, therefore, not to despise
anyone, as if they were beneath me; not
to bear a grudge against anyone who may
have done me wrong.

Whenever there is any work to be done for
the good of the parish, make me overcome
my laziness and my pride and give me the
desire to help.

Let me be a good example, not a stumbling
block, to those around me.

Prayer of Saint Francis

Lord, make me an instrument of your peace.

Where there is hatred let me sow peace;
where there is injury, pardon;
where there is doubt, let me sow faith;
where there is despair, let me give hope;
where there is darkness, let me give light;
where there is sadness, let me give joy.

O Divine Master, grant that I may not seek
to be comforted, but to comfort;
to be understood, but to understand;
to be loved, but to love.

For it is in giving that we receive,
it is in forgiving that we are forgiven,
and it is in dying
    that we are born to eternal life.

Prayer of St Richard

O dear Lord,
three things I pray:
to see thee more clearly,
love thee more dearly,
and follow thee more nearly,
day by day.

A Thought on Thanksgiving

It is very easy to pray to God
    when we are in trouble;
even people who do not think
    they believe in God
may utter a short prayer in times of crisis.
Fewer people thank God
    for the good things which we are given.
Remember how often Jesus said,
'Father, I thank you…'

Etta Gullick

INDEX